Y0-ART-111

Reading Spenser ❧
An Introduction to
The Faerie Queene

Reading Spenser

STUDIES IN LANGUAGE AND LITERATURE

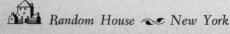 *Random House* ❧ *New York*

An
Introduction to
The 🙥
Faerie Queene

ROGER SALE

University of Washington

First Printing
© Copyright, 1968, by Random House, Inc.
All rights reserved under International and
Pan-American Copyright Conventions. Published in New York
by Random House, Inc. and simultaneously in Toronto, Canada,
by Random House of Canada Limited.
Library of Congress Catalog Card Number: 68-13466
Manufactured in the United States of America
by The Colonial Press Inc., Clinton, Mass.
Typography by Leon Bolognese

For
THEODORE BAIRD

Acknowledgments

Chapter II, "Spenser's Undramatic Poetry," first appeared, in a somewhat different form, in *Elizabethan Poetry: Modern Essays in Criticism,* ed. Paul J. Alpers (New York: Oxford University Press, 1967).

A summer grant from the Dean of the Graduate School of the University of Washington in 1964 made it possible for me to write a draft of what eventually became this book. It was a golden summer, and I am very grateful for having been able to have it.

The book began long before that, however, during long and wayward conversations with John A. Cameron of Amherst College about what I called "undramatic" and he called "symbolic" poetry. The results of these conversations were then tried out with many students both at Amherst and at Washington, and from these trials I learned almost all I know about Spenser. Though the students are here anonymous, they are certainly not so in my mind.

Paul Alpers of the University of California at Berkeley and Anne Howells of Occidental College have read the manuscript at almost every stage. Their severity and enthusiasm have been my major means of locomotion, and to have had such an audience, especially at those times when mistiness seemed the only alternative to clumsiness, has been a great blessing indeed.

Finally, my wife Dorothy typed the manuscript and in the process tightened and straightened it a great deal, thereby keeping things going beautifully just when it seemed that not only the book but the author was finished.

Seattle, Washington   R. S.
March, 1967

Contents

Reading Spenser ~
An Introduction to
The Faerie Queene

I ❧ Introduction

The Faerie Queene is one of the marvels of our culture. It is sometimes thought of as being old or old-
fashioned, but what it really is is unique, the longest
poem in English, perhaps the greatest as well, an immense
and seemingly endless series of stanzas filled with knights
and ladies, castles and bowers. It counts among its admirers almost every major poet from Sir Philip Sidney to
Tennyson, and it exerts on any who once begin to move
with its stately motions a charm and a compelling force
which no other poem can equal. Its author, Edmund
Spenser, does not seem in himself to be a very attractive
figure, and his other work, almost without exception, is
minor indeed. Yet those who know *The Faerie Queene*
never worry about these matters; for them the one huge

poem is enough to make its author live, with Shakespeare
as his only obvious peer.

Yet it is not a poem many people read. There was, in
centuries before our own, a sense in which an educated
man felt as obliged to read it as to read the major works
of Chaucer, Milton, or Wordsworth, but it has never been
a truly popular work; perhaps few in any age have read
it simply because they wanted to. In the last century,
furthermore, fewer and fewer people have tried to maintain its status as one of our major poems. A great deal is
written on *The Faerie Queene,* to be sure, but most of it
is written by professional Spenserians for other professional Spenserians. Many students of English literature,
including specialists in Renaissance poetry, feel no need
to read or reread beyond Book I and the most famous
cantos. Makers of anthologies are content with choosing
one or two obvious high spots. Survey courses that would
not consider leaving out a play of Marlowe's or Webster's
consider Spenser's poem only in passing. Thus it is gradually becoming another of those huge, unfinished, and
generally forgotten works that belongs as much in the
same company with Drayton's *Poly-Olbion* as it does
with Milton's *Paradise Lost.* As long ago as 1931 T. S.
Eliot felt it could be rather safely dismissed:

. . . for who, except scholars, and except the eccentric
few who are born with a sympathy for such work, or
others who have deliberately studied themselves into
the right appreciation, can now read through the whole
of *The Faerie Queene* with delight? [1]

Five years later a critic almost as influential as Eliot,
F. R. Leavis, added: "Spenser, in his own way a fact of

[1] *Selected Essays* (New York: Harcourt, Brace, 1932), p. 441.

the first importance in the tradition of English poetry, is too simple a fact to need examining afresh." [2] Further-more, after Eliot and Leavis made these dismissing re-marks, no one objected. It must be assumed that their audiences agreed with them.

Most readers first coming to *The Faerie Queene* do feel they are about to enter the preserve of scholars and "the eccentric few who are born with a sympathy for such work." They have been told it is an allegory, massive and requiring immense learning to be read. That learning, furthermore, is about a world that for most of us is dead. Spenser's language is deliberately archaic, his manners cannot be ruffled by modern questioning, his received universe is Christian and classical, his certainty is so com-plete that it strikes many on first blush as being only naive. Most of us do not, in the strict sense, "agree" with Spenser or his view of the world, and, sensing this, many have felt after reading a little way into the poem that what is involved in understanding it is an effort far too great for the average reader who is willing to work hard only if he feels that his labors will be rewarded with literary pleasure. The characters are flat, the episodes are apt to be long and seldom are what we usually think of as carefully connected, the poetry is generally unexciting, and the poet is apt to seem a simple-minded moralist who finds endless pleasure in praising obvious good and in denouncing obvious evil. For many readers the only way to imagine that this can be great poetry is to imagine that one must drop his usual frame of mind and carefully study oneself into the right mood and come equipped with the right learning. Most editions of *The Faerie Queene* are replete with notes citing sources and echoes from Homer, Virgil, Ovid, the Bible, Plato, Aristotle,

[2] *Revaluation* (London: Chatto and Windus, 1936), p. 5.

Ariosto, Tasso, medieval rhetorical theory, and Elizabethan politics. The ordinary wary reader can perhaps be excused for believing that he has no chance with the poem unless he comes equipped knowing all that Spenser apparently knew.

This book is written with two convictions: first, that *The Faerie Queene* is a very great poem, at least as great as its admirers claim, and second, that it is a poem which can be read and enjoyed, perhaps greatly, by students of literature with no great store of learning and with no special sympathy for Spenser's official beliefs. About the "learning" problem the best thing to be said immediately is that Spenser, unlike Chaucer and often unlike Shakespeare, almost never alludes to something without explaining it or making it his own, so that the only way to find out what Spenser thinks about Adonis or the Book of Revelation is to read the poem rather than something else. About Spenser's official beliefs—in a received and revealed organic and harmonious universe—the best thing to be said first is that Spenser is not most interesting for his beliefs but for his sense of life, and Spenser's sense of life is finally not something that most modern readers find very strange. About the allegory perhaps the best thing to be said is that there is nothing the least difficult or obscure about it; what Spenser means is almost always exactly what he says—compared to Shakespeare he is an "easy" poet indeed. What is required of a reader of *The Faerie Queene* is neither learning, nor beliefs, nor an "allegorical frame of mind" (whatever that may be), but only what is required of a reader of any very long work: time and patience. The commentary that follows assumes nothing more of its readers. My own experience, plus that of many others, has convinced me that the way to understand Spenser is to read the poem all the way through.

This by itself is a large undertaking, of course, but everyone who has done it can attest to the security and thoroughness of his instinctive knowledge of the way of Faerie Land. There are places in the poem where the intent or meaning will seem obscure, though most will come near the beginning when the reader is still unfamiliar with the poem's ways. But the places that indeed do require something in the way of extra knowledge are only stanzas or groups of stanzas here and there; for almost its entire length one finds out how to read the poem by reading it. What is hard about *The Faerie Queene* is getting used to the kind of poem it is. We need to discover how it differs from other poems and requires shifts in our expectations about character and narrative. But once we begin to know it for the thing it is, *The Faerie Queene* becomes stately, luminous, and finally irreplaceable.

To do justice to Edmund Spenser, then, we must first try to see what kind of poem it is he wrote, then try to explore critically some of its dimensions and boundaries. The poem's partisans generally agree we need to understand its aims or intentions first, yet often they seem to feel that once we have done that the whole poem seems good because it seems clear. But it seems to me unjust to Spenser to claim that his poem is always and everywhere equally good, for unless we find ways of defining what is wrong with the poem when it is wrong, we will never have ways of praising the poem for its greatest achievements. To try to do justice is to assume detachment rather than partisanship, and the only way we can remain detached is to remember constantly that we are whoever it is we are, asking of literature that it be vital for us. The judgments arrived at here are those of a skeptical and interested reader convinced of Spenser's greatness and convinced that the only decent homage one can pay to greatness is to find one's own terms for praise and condemnation. It is fruitless, always, to ask what Spenser would have made of what we say about him; we must speak in our voice as he spoke in his. If the imagination and literary criticism count for anything, they show that just as we do not have to be Spenserians in order to read *The Faerie Queene,* neither do we have to pretend an interest in what we find boring nor hide an excitement because it seems strange and unlikely.

I have not tried to write a book covering all Spenser's work, and often I speak of *The Faerie Queene* as "Spenser's poem" as though it were all he ever wrote. Despite many efforts made on behalf of one or another of the minor poems, the experience of most readers is that except for the *Epithalamion* and one or two of the *Amoretti* sonnets, *The Faerie Queene* is what we have of his that can genuinely engage our interest. I have not even tried to "cover" *The Faerie Queene.* That has been done, from varying points of view, quite often of late, and what I try to do here has not. We need to arrive at a point where critical distinctions can be made; if the poem's adherents are to assume it is all good and most of its would-be readers are a little afraid they will find it all bad or uninteresting, then some mediation between these two positions is necessary.

But, to repeat, understanding must precede criticism, and here especially, because the major reason for Spenser's decline in popularity is misapprehension about the kind of poem he wrote. The next chapter, then, on "undramatic" poetry, tries to provide a way of seeing the poem that accounts for its most essential features: its quietness, its narrative and rhetorical methods, its length, its serene inclusiveness. These *are* strange to us because our expectations about literature have been created for us by what I call the "dramatic" writing of Shakespeare and the great novelists. I place the emphasis on the "undramatic" quality of the poem in part to avoid what seems to me general and unnecessary perturbation about the nature of its allegory, that quality which is usually assumed to distinguish it from most later poems. Here are some statements which show the traditional approaches to the problem:

> . . . for, whatever may be true of some other poets, the aesthetic patterning of Spenser and Milton is based upon ideas, upon conceptual thinking.

> The governing principle of Spenser's poem is intellectual and thematic rather than narrative, dramatic, or symbolic.

> The development . . . is not "dramatic" or "novelistic"; it is thematic and allegorical.

I want to return to these statements in the next chapter and treat them in somewhat greater detail; here let it suffice to say that all three are trying to make clear that *The Faerie Queene* is not the same kind of work as *Hamlet* or *Tom Jones*. But the way they stress the differences is unfortunate. If we insist on the themes, the ideas, and the way the allegory extends the dark conceit, we almost inevitably move towards a sense of Spenser's meaning that is best stated as a series of abstractions. Yet the closer we come to summary sentences which begin with phrases like "Holiness is . . ." or "Prince Arthur represents . . ." the closer we come, inevitably, to thinking of Spenser as a writer of commonplaces and schoolboy maxims. In a very real sense "holiness" or "temperance" or "chastity" were to Spenser what tradition had always

said they were, and if we seek to find in the poem some
new and different sense of "the meaning of holiness," we
will probably be sorely disappointed. It is essential to say
that the subject of Book I is *not* the Red Crosse Knight
or Una or Duessa, and that the subject *is* holiness or the
spiritual lot of men; it is also essential to add that the
characters and scenes in *The Faerie Queene* are Spenser's
means rather than his ends. But this does not mean that
his ends are abstract definitions. If all we seek are those,
one or two cantos in each book will more than suffice.

I need to add a note here about my emphasis on the
poem's length. One of the unique facts about *The Faerie
Queene* is that it is theoretically endless. Of course it
does have an end, but that is not the point. As we read
we are always aware of the way it goes on and on and
on, and this awareness conditions in large measure the
way we read it and think about it and try to hold it in
our minds. With other long poems we read expecting to
find what we find in most long novels—a sense of direction, of climaxes, a sense of completeness. But this is
hardly true of *The Faerie Queene*; we can find no stanza
or canto to which we can point and say, "Here is the
climax, the point towards which we have been moving
all along." Characters and places come in and go out of
our vision without remark. Some reappear just as we left
them, some reappear in altered form, some are gone forever; we can never tell what is going to happen in the
next episode, or how, or to whom. In stressing this point
I may seem to imply that the poem is therefore meander-
ing or boring, so long that only a fool or a hero would
finish it. But I mean nothing of the sort. To say the poem
is theoretically endless is to imply neither praise nor
blame; it is only to begin to ask how a poem that is so

even and apparently monotonous in tone and method could be so very fascinating.

After establishing a general idea of undramatic poetry I turn to the way the "undrama" is created, beginning at the local level of diction and syntax because it is there we constantly confront Spenser's characteristic ways of thinking and writing. In most poems the relation of adjectives to nouns is simple, but in *The Faerie Queene* it is often maddening and exciting. The looseness of the syntax, the countless tiny ambiguities, the shifts in phrase and tone that give the poem its sense of celebration— these are the bases for everything else: the story, the allegory, the "meaning." As Spenser works with phrase and sentence, so he works with narrative and large allegorical effect, and until we confront the looseness and the undismayed flexibility in the smallest matters, we will probably be tempted to call the work as a whole inconsistent, incoherent, and confused. As one reads the details make the frame, not the other way around, so proceeding from details and building up a sense of the large effects reduces the constant danger of making the poem give back to us the form and meaning we impose on it. Perhaps a single non-Spenserian example here will clarify what I mean by loose syntax. Here are the opening lines of Keats' "La Belle Dame Sans Merci":

> *Ah what can ail thee, wretched wight*
> *Alone and palely loitering?*

Readers have found these lines memorable for a century without ever having felt the need to ask about the grammatical relation of "palely" to "loitering." We recognize the effect long before we feel compelled to search for a

cause. But surely, though "palely" is technically an adverb modifying "loitering," the phrase by itself makes
little sense; seeing this we can search for explanations but
will probably find that the best we can say is that "palely"
is a word which modifies every other word in the sentence
and, indeed, gives the lines their distinct coloration by so
doing. This is admittedly a striking example, and what
makes it striking is its uncommonness in Keats and almost every other post-Shakespearean poet. But things like
this are happening in almost every stanza of *The Faerie
Queene*. We are not twenty stanzas into the poem before
we come on this line: "His gall did grate for griefe and
high disdaine." Again, following our normal sense of
syntax, we say that "grate" covers both "griefe" and "disdaine." We quickly see that this is not so, that what
Spenser means is that the Red Crosse Knight's gall grated
for grief and he also or subsequently felt high disdain.
Here the example, though the usage is perhaps even odder
than in Keats' lines quoted above, seems less striking when
read in context, because things like this appear almost
everywhere. The loose or flexible syntax, then, is our first
sign of our undramatic writer, and we can move from
this, as we do while reading, out to larger concerns of
story, meaning, and organization.

If this procedure is at all illuminating, then commentary on the poem should simply begin with the first stanza
and watch the poem take shape right through to the end.
One result of doing this, by the way, would be to become
aware of how much in the poem has never received comment, at least in print. That is the inevitable result of the
traditional stress on the abstract quality of the allegory
which has led critics to place great emphasis on some
stanzas and episodes while others have gone unremarked.
But as a practical matter, commenting on every stanza is

impossible, so I have, in the third chapter, effected a com-
promise by discussing a single book as a sequence. Ideally
the chapter would be read by someone working along in
Book III by himself and checking his impressions of the
way the book takes shape against mine. If nothing else,
such a reader would see how much, often how very much,
even a fairly thorough commentary leaves out. I chose
Book III for this purpose for a number of reasons which
deserve mention because most readers begin with Book I
and often read no more than that. Book III seems to me
the best of the completed six, and the last four cantos
of the book represent the longest stretch of unbroken
great writing in this or perhaps in any poem. But in
addition Book III provides instance after instance of the
way in which Spenser works to make flat and apparently
undistinguished poetry seem precise and, because precise,
beautiful. Spenser is not often a quotable poet, yet when
his sense of his sequence and his vision are as secure as
they are for most of Book III, he writes poetry with its
own kind of greatness. Finally, I chose Book III because
it is the best example in the poem of Spenser's ability to
organize and control his sequence, so that we need not
look for coherence or consistency of narrative or characterization in order to find mastery of technique and
organization.

The last chapter is on Books V and VI. It is my sense
that something happened to Spenser during the 1590's
while he was working on the second set of three books,
something that forced him to change some of the poem's
fundamental techniques and methods. The world on
which the poem looks in Book VI is a far more "dramatic"
place than the Faerie Land of the earlier parts of the
poem. By showing an urgent and shaken Spenser here,
we can see how the poem changed from a work that is

theoretically endless to a work Spenser could not finish; we can also find a way, perhaps, to measure the secure and serene poet who conceived Books I–IV. For the historian of literature the landscape of the end of Book V and all of Book VI is a fascinating place, for we see there, I think, the last and greatest medieval poet becoming a "modern," so to speak. It might be part of our praise of the poet, if not, strictly speaking, of the poem, that in shifting from Faerie Land to pastoral countryside Spenser was aware of something deep and abiding that was happening to English culture. Spenser could never make his poem respond to this change in his world as Shakespeare was able to make his drama do, but at the very least it can be said that the great Shakespearean heroes, the architects of our "dramatic" modern world, are all exiles from Faerie Land even as Spenser himself finally was.

If we can understand what happened to *The Faerie Queene*, furthermore, we should be in a position to see why it has become increasingly difficult for readers to understand the Faerie that is Spenser's great achievement, for the processes at work to create this difficulty were at work even as Spenser wrote Books V and VI. We implicitly recognize this fact whenever we sense that Spenser is of an era too early for us while Shakespeare, especially the Shakespeare of the tragedies and romances, is not. I do not, as I have said, believe that Spenser's poem is of an age too early for us, but I can easily understand how and why readers have difficulty gaining their bearings in *The Faerie Queene*, a poem of crystalline clarity, who have no trouble feeling at home in such wild and improbable works as *King Lear* and *Macbeth*.

C. S. Lewis has said that to attempt an agreed estimate about *The Faerie Queene* is now futile. It may well be that to attempt an agreed estimate about any work is futile, but it is also true that such an estimate of Spenser is going to grow more rather than less difficult as time goes on. Lewis himself was "of" Spenser's world in the narrow as well as the broad sense—he believed as Spenser believed as well as read his poem with pleasure—and he perhaps inevitably felt that those on the other side of the chasm, those who do not believe as Spenser believed, could never understand his poem. Perhaps inevitably also, Lewis saw nothing going wrong with the poem in the last two books. But to think this way is to underestimate the poem, really, by assuming that we really do need Spenser's sense of the world in order to love his poem— Spenser's imagination is both deeper and wider than that. But chasms have formed, some readers are Christians who believe in a received and revealed universe and some are not, some have a temperamental affinity for knightly romance and some do not, some instinctively delight in fairy worlds because they seem remote, and some are repelled from them for precisely the same reason. Given this, it may seem strange that I speak throughout of someone called "the reader," when in fact I should be facing the fact that perhaps "the reader" is only me. Of course all readers are different readers, and some are more learned, more sensitive, more pious, more delighted by monsters than others. But the "reader" I speak of is, I hope, a reader of no particular temperamental affinities one way or the other. He is, to be sure, a fiction, assembled as he is from my own reading, from the reading of others, and from my sense of the ideal reader implied by the poem itself. The reader I speak of, then, is no extraordinary beast; by and large he is only a patient and willing man. Reading *The Faerie Queene* requires time because it is very long. The poem must be read piecemeal—a few cantos at a time—for after that, in almost everyone's experience, the poem begins to blur. It requires patience because of its even tone and stately movement, and anyone who reads hurriedly will not be able to see what is happening.

To return to a statement made at the beginning of this introduction, *The Faerie Queene* will never be a widely read poem. We can see why if we compare it to the other great long poem in English, *Paradise Lost,* to which it is most obviously comparable in scope and stature. The figure of Milton, though many find it repellent, is sufficiently large, crabbed, and heroic to make him an attractive figure for many who do not, in the sense I have been using the term, "agree" with Milton. Many have sensed great internal struggles within the poet and his epic and have tried to show that *Paradise Lost* is the result of poetic and doctrinal immovable objects meeting historically irresistible forces that make the poem fascinating, if only because they show the strength of a poet trying to overpower or deny difficulties. Others have replied that it is a work far more intricate and carefully imagined than any detractor could realize—and so the debate has continued. But no one senses any such interesting difficulties with the almost anonymous figure of Spenser. One critic writes:

> Spenser's ideas are quite . . . dead . . . but they do not interfere . . . with the patterns of his poetry; the reason is not altogether that Spenser's art is dead too, but that his ideas and feelings formed a more or less tractable synthesis to which his style was truly answerable.[3]

[3] Robert M. Adams, *Ikon* (Ithaca: Cornell University Press, 1955), p. 216.

Spenser's ideas are dead, his art is dead, but the two are dead harmoniously—such seems to be the argument, and inevitably such an argument leads to the sense that Eliot was right and that only very special people quite unlike ourselves could ever enjoy *The Faerie Queene*. Spenser's ideas and feelings did form a tractable synthesis to which his style was truly answerable, but that should be a mark of excellence even if it is also a reason for his being little read. For, in a sense I will explore near the end of the book, Milton—to say nothing of Blake and Shelley—would have done precisely as Spenser did had they been able. They would not have written poems like *The Faerie Queene*, to be sure, but they often tried to be as undramatic, as serenely visionary, as Spenser in fact was. If we prefer heroic doubt to confident vision, well and good, but in doing so we must admit that the preference is not the least based on an idea of literary excellence and is probably only a sign of imaginative limitation in ourselves.

For the reward of *The Faerie Queene* is imaginative release and subsequent recognition of a different sense of our human condition. It is not escape at all, for Faerie Land is not a happy place and its heroes finally can accomplish little more than we do ourselves. The release is offered by a poet who knows what we know about life but who sees its context and implications very differently. Holiness, temperance, chastity—the words are old-fashioned and the ideas they embody are not really alive—but if these virtues are the subject of the poem, they are not its reason for being. Spenser may have been trying to fashion the idea of a gentleman, but what he achieved was something quite different and, for most of us, far more interesting. The poem offers a world created by a poet who knew what he knew so clearly that he did not, in the narrow sense, have to think or to rise to an allegorical "level" of abstraction in order to express his knowing. Of course we do not live in such a world; no one ever did. But we can all go there.

❧

Notes on Spenser's life and work, especially for those reading The Faerie Queene for the first time.

Edmund Spenser was born in 1552, in London, and went to the school of the Merchant Tailors there in 1560. While there he apparently began writing poetry, and his first appearance in print is as an anonymous translator of a Dutch poem, Van der Noot's *Theatre* (1569). In that year Spenser also matriculated at Pembroke Hall, Cambridge, where he remained until 1576. He then became secretary to Bishop Young of Rochester and he was a confidential emissary to the Earl of Leicester in 1579 at which time he met Sir Philip Sidney. His first published work under his own name, *The Shepheardes Calender*, appeared in the same year, but many marginal glosses in that work indicate that Spenser had already written more besides, and much of this we know only by title. He had written two of what later became the *Fowre Hymnes*, "The Teares of the Muses" (mostly translations from Latin and French), "Virgils Gnat," a version of "Mother Hubberds Tale," and almost certainly material that was later incorporated into *The Faerie Queene*. The *Calender* was a considerable success and Spenser clearly hoped to gain a court appointment from it, but none was forthcoming, and in 1580 he left England as secretary to

Arthur Lord Grey of Wilton, the Queen's deputy in Ireland. From this time on he was a virtual exile.

In the summer of 1589 Sir Walter Raleigh visited
Ireland and met Spenser. Raleigh found the poet of the
Calender living virtually unknown and at work on a
huge and major poem, *The Faerie Queene*. In 1590
Spenser and Raleigh returned to England and the first
three books of the poem were published at the end of
that year. To these Spenser appended the usual dedica-
tory and commendatory verses and a letter to Raleigh
which outlines his plan for his poem as he then saw it.
He returned to Ireland in 1591 after leaving behind more
minor poems, many of them fifteen years old, published
as the *Complaints, Muiopotmos, Daphnaïda*. His verse
record of his journey to England, *Colin Clouts Come
Home Againe* (Colin Clout was the name Spenser had
used for himself in the *Calender*), was published in 1595.
In 1594 Spenser married Elizabeth Boyle, to whom are
written the *Amoretti* sonnets and Spenser's one fine short
work, the *Epithalamion*; these were published together in
1595. In the next year came Books IV–VI of *The Faerie
Queene*, the *Prothalamion*, and the *Fowre Hymnes*. He
returned to England late in the fall of 1598 and died at
Westminster in 1599. In 1608 were published *Two
Cantos of Mutabilitie* which have been labeled, for con-
venience's sake, a fragment of Book VII. When they
were written or where they were intended to appear in
the poem is unknown.

The "Letter of the Authors" to Sir Walter Raleigh is
prefixed to all substantial selections and complete editions of *The Faerie Queene*, and readers are advised to
read it carefully. But what it reveals is Spenser's intentions in 1590, and the poem, even the part published with

the letter, contradicts these intentions in many places. Spenser has envisaged a poem in twelve books—"The generall end therefore of all the booke is to fashion a gentleman or noble person in vertuous and gentle discipline," and his means for achieving this end is chivalric romance. But most readers will find that the poem does not really feel the way the letter makes it seem, and there is no particular reason why anyone should read the poem so as to make it fit the poem apparently described in the letter. The poem is organized, of course, but not really in the fashion of the letter.

Because Spenser saw his poem through the press and no manuscripts of it survive, there are no major editorial problems of the sort that fascinate and plague readers of Shakespeare or other Elizabethan dramatists. Almost any edition of the poem will suffice. The fullest and most authoritative is *The Works of Edmund Spenser*[:] *A Variorum Edition,* ed. Greenlaw, Osgood, Padelford, and Heffner, et al. (Baltimore, 1932–1949) in ten volumes. To this edition is appended the best life of Spenser, by A. C. Judson. The notes and commentary here give an almost complete account of all work published on Spenser at the time the edition was done. Because the *Variorum* is to all intents and purposes available only in libraries, my quotations and references are to the best popularly priced edition, *The Complete Poetical Works of Spenser,* ed. R. E. Neil Dodge (Boston, 1908). The print in this edition is rather small, but very large compared to the only other that includes the complete poem, the one in the Oxford Standard Authors series. A single columned text of the poem in one volume has never been done and is sorely needed.

Work on Spenser is voluminous and the beginner is advised to avoid it entirely until he has read a good deal of the poem. By far the best way to learn how to read *The Faerie Queene,* for reasons I try to make clear later, is to read the poem all the way through; any commentary is secondary after that. But for those to whom this is not possible, two introductions (other than this book) can be mentioned. The first is the commentary of C. S. Lewis in *The Allegory of Love* (Oxford, 1936), pp. 297–360, and in *English Literature in the Sixteenth Century* (Oxford, 1954), pp. 347–393. Lewis can be very misleading but he is always witty and readable and his enthusiasm for Spenser has infected many readers. The second is the section devoted to Spenser in Paul Alpers' collection, *Elizabethan Poetry: Modern Essays in Criticism* (Oxford, 1967). Of course there is a great deal in the literature on Spenser that will be of help and interest to many readers, but it is difficult to say just what work will help whom. The one item that deserves special mention, if only because it is not generally known, is the brilliant passage on the Spenserian stanza in William Empson's *Seven Types of Ambiguity,* 3rd ed. (New York, 1955), pp. 40–42.

II ❧ Spenser's Undramatic Poetry

The Faerie Queene is not a "difficult" poem in the sense that "The Extasie" or "The Garden" or "Le Monocle de Mon Oncle" are "difficult" poems, but readers unquestionably do have a difficult time getting used to it and coming to know what to make of it. It is not the poem itself, though, that is hard, but the expectations of most readers, about what poetry, narrative, and characterization are or should be, are apt to stand in the way of any easy comprehension of it. I want to begin with one set of expectations readers often have, those surrounding the words "dramatic" and "undramatic," and try to find ways of describing Spenser's poetry as the undramatic verse it is. If, as sometimes happens, we assume that "dramatic" is a term of praise—when someone says *King Lear* or *Wuthering Heights* are "very dramatic" we assume they mean, among other things, that these works are "very good"—then "undramatic" will probably imply flatness, monotony, and flaccidity, in which case Spenser will seem an undramatic writer guilty of all these faults. If, however, we can come to see "dramatic" and "undramatic" simply as two different ways of looking at the world, then *The Faerie Queene,* which is so obviously bad dramatic poetry, may begin to seem great poetry of a quite different kind.

Originally the word "dramatic" referred only to literary works that were performed on the stage, and "undramatic" described a work that was not suitable for acting. In time, however, "dramatic" began to mean "exciting" and, at the same time, "theatrical" began to mean "artificial" or "trumped up." Thus "dramatic" meant something better than the thrills of a simple melodrama, a more elevated kind of excitement than the mere trickery of clever staging could produce. "Dramatic" also came to be used as a more strictly literary term to describe moments, events, passages, and even whole works in which there were genuine and grand confrontations between discrete and clearly defined characters. In the novel the omniscient narrator gave way to one who was himself a participant in the action, and a "dramatic" novel was not only one in which the action was scenic and approximated action on a stage, but one in which the mystery created by human confrontation was not sullied by a director constantly telling the audience what to look at and how to think. Historically, then, as our sense of the failure or absence of higher powers in the universe increased, so did our implied praise of "dramatic" works in which the human agents were left alone to face each other and their destinies. At the same time *The Faerie Queene,* which is obviously not dramatic in this sense, began to seem old or old-fashioned, sport for "the eccentric few who are born with a sympathy for such work." What happened to our sense of Spenser happened as our sense of what is good or relevant changed. It may be true that the reader of *The Faerie Queene* finally needs only trust Spenser's verse in order to learn how to read it, but it is also true that most readers cannot do this without first becoming aware that long before they ever came to Spenser many dramatic works created their sense of what poetry should be.

In a dramatic work a character or a narrator speaks, but what he says is not the whole truth. Another character answers or the narrator takes a different position. What he says is not the whole truth either, but it clarifies for us what the first speaker did not and usually could not know. A gap appears between two characters or between character and narrator: Heathcliff speaks, Nelly Dean comments and we, as readers, know more than either will ever know; Claudius tries to pray but fails, and Hamlet, because he believes the prayer successful, vows his most demonic revenge. In what is probably the fullest and most explicit rendering of this dramatic sense of gaps between people, George Eliot in *Middlemarch* appeals to our "common sense" belief that each person is only his own candle held up to the random scratches on a pierglass:

> If to Dorothea Mr. Casaubon had been the mere occasion which had set alight the fine inflammable material of her youthful illusions, does it follow that he was fairly represented in the minds of those less impassioned personages who have hitherto delivered their judgments concerning him? I protest against any absolute conclusion, any prejudice derived from Mrs. Cadwallader's contempt for a neighbouring clergyman's

alleged greatness of soul, of Sir James Chettam's poor
opinion of his rival's legs,—from Mr. Brooke's failure
to solicit a companion's ideas, or from Celia's criticism
of a middle-aged scholar's personal appearance.

"I protest against any absolute conclusion" is the implicit
attitude of the writer of dramatic literature, and when
we look at the most highly praised passages in the literature of the last three centuries we find most often dramatic
moments that are supremely expressive of our sense of
the mystery in the human condition. The gaps create
irony and drama, and the author who makes us aware of
gaps earns our highest praise because we admire authors
who know they do not know all the answers.

It follows from this that in a dramatic work the story
will "really be a story," and it will shift and turn as the
characters' or the narrator's view of the world changes. An
omniscient narrator will work to maintain evenness of
tone and point of view; Thackeray, for example, has his
range in *Vanity Fair,* but once we have learned what the
range is, little that Becky or Amelia can do affects it
much. The book is governed by the idea of Vanity Fair,
and almost everything that happens serves to demonstrate
once again that all is vanity. But in a more dramatic work
like *Emma,* the narrator must change her stance at every
stage in the education of her heroine. At the beginning
Emma is very young, selfish, and blind, so the narrator
can be quite neat in her ironies, quite simple in her covert
disapproval. But a tone appropriate towards an Emma
who does not realize Mr. Elton is making love to her is
quite inappropriate towards an Emma recovering from
the humiliations of Box Hill. That is why, in a dramatic
work, context is so important. We cannot speak of Hamlet
without also specifying which Hamlet we mean, for the

Hamlet of the first soliloquy is not "the same man" as the Hamlet who asks Horatio to "absent thee from felicity awhile." Even in a work with only one character this is often true: in "Ode to the Nightingale" our sense of who "Keats" is depends almost entirely on where we are in the poem, for the "Ode" is a journey and the central figure shifts and turns much as does a Shakespearean tragic hero or a Jane Austen heroine.

If in a dramatic work we have clearly delineated characters created by gaps in understanding between each other and/or the narrator, if we have a story that renders the fullest possibilities of change as expressive of its sense of life, then an undramatic work is one in which no such striking change is possible, no marked differences among characters exist, no shifts in point of view occur. The author of a dramatic work is skeptical and uses his story to discover his sense of life. The author of an undramatic work is certain and does not need his story to discover a sense of life he already commands. The dramatic work expresses differences, usually discordances, while the undramatic work emphasizes likenesses, usually harmonies. Most undramatic authors are in some sense visionary; they know their world and move freely within its boundaries. C. S. Lewis has a description of Spenser that can serve as a preliminary definition of all undramatic writers:

> He discovered early the things he valued, and there is no sign that his allegiance ever wavered. He was of course often, perhaps usually, disappointed. The actual court did not conform to his standard of courtesy: mutability, if philosophically accepted from the outset, might yet prove unexpectedly bitter to the taste. But disappointment is not necessarily conflict. It did not for Spenser discredit the things of which he was disappointed. It

might breed melancholy, or indignation, but not doubt.
. . . He was often sad: but not, at bottom, worried.[1]

Of all the major English poets Spenser is perhaps the
most undramatic, or most consistently so. For later undramatic poets who had anything like Spenser's genius
had to face, at least implicitly, what Spenser did not have
to face until the end of his career. Spenser inherited a
view of the universe that was still harmonious and still
able to engender a common culture which gave him all
the materials he needed. But for Milton, Blake, and
Shelley (to name only the most obvious examples) the
inheritance was increasingly less secure because historical
forces were at work to create an increasingly secular,
skeptical, dramatic world. The language, imagery, and
revelation quite easily available to Spenser was technically
still "there" for Milton, but Milton could not work at
ease with these materials, for what he believed and what
he saw were not always the same or even reconcilable.
By the time of Blake and Shelley the visionary poet was
driven more and more to private language, in the case of
Blake, and to ecstatic mistiness, in the case of Shelley, in
order to maintain the primacy of the vision. For a critic
like F. R. Leavis, who looks for poetic language really
used by men, these poets are bound to be seen as having
paid too high a price. Dr. Leavis has "history" on his side
and his Great Tradition of more dramatic authors has
been the mainstream of our literature since the death of
Spenser and the decisive force of Shakespeare.

Anyone who comes to *The Faerie Queene* having been,
in effect, raised on Shakespeare, Donne, and (what is

---

[1] *English Literature in the Sixteenth Century* (Oxford: Oxford
University Press, 1954), p. 392.

more likely) the novel is almost certainly going to be baffled and annoyed at first. Many put it down after a few cantos or one book as a work lifeless and probably confused. For, after all, if one is looking for scenes, for characters, even for allegory as clearly articulated as it is in *Pilgrim's Progress,* then *The Faerie Queene* is hopeless. There is no "there" *there,* to use a phrase of Gertrude Stein's, and furthermore, Spenser seems totally undisturbed by this fact. On and on it goes, battles, castles, streams, and tapestries, with never more than a slight break in the monotonous evenness of the tone. There is no consistency to the narrative, no coherent fictional world, and little in the way of causal connections between episodes. In the second canto of the first book the Red Crosse Knight, while riding on the plain with Duessa, meets a tree named Fradubio that tells him its story; in the third canto Una, separated from the Knight, meets Abessa, Kirkrapine, a lion, and Sansloy; in the fourth canto the Red Crosse Knight and Duessa go to the House of Pride. None of these events is related causally to another. We cannot say where the Red Crosse Knight is while Una is outside Abessa's cottage with the lion. We cannot say how the Red Crosse Knight happens to find Fradubio or how far he goes or in what direction he travels in order to go from Fradubio to the House of Pride. We say that one event happens "after" another because they are arranged in a sequence, but we cannot locate any reason, as far as the "career" of the Knight is concerned, why he could not go first to the House of Pride and then meet Fradubio, or why he could not have done both these things before Una meets Sansloy. There *is* something like a story in Book I but if we try to organize our sense of the book around that story, then these three events will begin to seem irrelevant.

Book I, furthermore, has much more sense of story than any of the other five. Characters come and go unannounced and undescribed, good fights endlessly against evil, the poem goes on forever. It never "gets anywhere."

Now those who know and love the poem know better than this in one sense, but often, in trying to explain to the skeptical or uninitiated why someone looking for a dramatic work is looking for the wrong things, they turn to the allegory, the thought, the conceptual framework:

> . . . for, whatever may be true of some other poets, the aesthetic patterning of Spenser and Milton is based upon ideas, upon conceptual thinking.[2]

> The governing principle of Spenser's poems is intellectual and thematic rather than narrative, dramatic, or symbolic.[3]

> The development . . . is not "dramatic" or "novelistic"; it is thematic and allegorical.[4]

The emphasis in Spenserian studies has always been on the themes, the ideas, and the way the allegory extends the dark conceit.

To some extent this emphasis is correct and unavoidable. Spenser certainly is not dramatic or novelistic and, if we are careful with the way we place the stress, Spenser's aesthetic patterning is *based upon* ideas. But still, those who are bored with the poem have a point too, and one most Spenserians ignore. Their sense is that the ideas

[2] A. S. P. Woodhouse, "Nature and Grace in *The Faerie Queene*," *ELH*, 16 (1949), 197.
[3] William Nelson, *The Poetry of Edmund Spenser* (New York: Columbia University Press, 1963), p. vii.
[4] Thomas P. Roche, Jr., *The Kindly Flame* (Princeton: Princeton University Press, 1964), p. 52.

in *The Faerie Queene* are commonplaces and that the poem seems not so much a large intellectual framework as an endless series of the same or similar events. In one sense the governing principles seem too obvious, apparent in every stanza. In another sense they seem hopelessly lost in a jungle of words. It is for this reason that I want to call *The Faerie Queene* undramatic rather than thematic or allegorical. It is quite clear, from internal evidence and from the Letter to Raleigh, that Spenser had at some stages of the composition an extremely vast structure in mind. But the emphasis should be on its vastness rather than on its structure. Whatever the frame, it had to allow for as many shifts in apparent direction as there are shifts in syntax, characterization, and narrative. For what holds *The Faerie Queene* together, and here the enemies of the poem seem more correct than its friends, is not so much a conceptual idea as a state of mind. No matter how long one has been away from the poem, no matter where one picks it up, no matter how long one reads, it always seems the same.

It should not be concluded, however, that there is no coherence in the poem or that one can rearrange the stanzas, cantos, or books and end up with the same poem. Just because the story of Britomart exists as a narrative independently of the story of the Squire of Dames (to say nothing of the stories of Guyon or Calidore), just because in some ways the story of Britomart in the Castle Joyeous exists independently of her subsequent rescue of Amoret, the poem is not therefore a hodgepodge. But in a poem as long, as even in tone, as repetitious in its events, the major organizing fact is going to be sequence, pure and simple. In a dramatic work, as we have seen, context, the specific stage of the story in question, is extremely important as one quotes and discusses character, tone, or atmosphere. In *The Faerie Queene* we move from forest to castle, from the House of Pride to the cave of Orgoglio, from defeat to triumph, but Spenser writes as though none of these events had any effect on his tone or manner. This evenness does a great deal to make *The Faerie Queene* among the hardest of poems for a reader to remember the sequence of events. Ask a man who is reading through as quickly as time and energy allow and who is in the middle of Book IV the following questions: "What is the name of the bloody-handed babe and when does he appear?" "Does Belphoebe rescue Timias before or after the witch remembers the false Florimell?" The chances are good that, even if he has read the poem before, he will blink, back off, smile, try to rub thoughts of Lust or Corflambo from his mind, and slowly go about piecing together the things which seemed so indelibly clear just a brief while ago. Nine out of ten readers in the midst of Book VI cannot remember if it was Artegall or Arthur who fought the Soldan in Book V. Whatever the structure, whatever the large-scale organization, Spenser has deliberately militated against our being aware as we read of much more than the preceding few cantos. The large formal structure of the poem is almost never the operative structure of the reader. For this reason Spenserian commentary even at its best often seems rather unreal, drawn as it is from the detached impulse to make the poem diagrammatic rather than from the experience of reading the poem.

For instance, in a recent book A. C. Hamilton outlines what seems a very persuasive argument that the structure of the extant six books repeats the structure of Book I.[5] He divides Book I into four sections, then says that these

[5] *The Structure of the Allegory in "The Faerie Queene"* (Oxford: Clarendon Press, 1961), pp. 148ff.

"contain the action of the whole poem"—the Red Crosse Knight's fall is repeated in Book II, his redemption by Arthur is repeated in Britomart's rescue of Amoret in Book III, his regeneration by Una is treated in Books IV and V, and his restoration after slaying the dragon is handled again in Book VI. A reader of Book I may feel there is something arbitrary in Mr. Hamilton's divisions of the stages of its action, but they certainly are defensible. But what Mr. Hamilton is in effect doing is saying that the reader must be aware of these particular stages of Book I as he is reading the rest of the poem. But when that reader tries to keep such a large and detailed structure in his head, he simply fails to read what is in front of him and ends convinced that either he or it should not be there. The effort to make patterns inevitably tends to flatten and simplify the myriad shifting details of the endless stanzas. Of course one must organize one's experience as a reader no matter how formless Spenser seems determined to make it. But that assertion of formal organization which cannot be made part of one's experience with the poem is bound to seem beside the point. Over and over in Spenserian commentary we are asked to compare the Garden of Adonis with the Temple of Venus, or the Bower of Bliss with the Castle of Busirane. But we can make such comparisons only long after we have finished the poem and we go back to discover, in a detached way, what it all means, where it is all going. The Garden of Adonis is in the middle of Book III and the Temple of Venus is near the end of Book IV, so that if we take them and put them side by side, we are making the structure, not Spenser. In the poem they are six thousand lines apart.

What we need, then, is a commentary that relies more fully on the sequence of the stanzas as they are on the page, that relies on using as our means of expressing the poem's meaning the sequence which is all a full-scale undramatic work can have for its main means of conveying meaning. Here is another example of recent Spenserian criticism which reveals beautifully how important sequence is and how distorted the poem seems when we ignore it:

> Over against the completely determinate ideal of Medina we have the mysterious three-dimensional ideal of Belphoebe. Belphoebe's instinctive and natural mode of temperance is contrasted to Medina's primarily rational moderation; her instinctive aloofness balances Medina's almost frenetic social concern.[6]

This seems to me both precise and persuasive and gives us a way that is also Spenser's way to "place" the flatness of the House of Medina in Book II, Canto ii. What Mr. Berger has done is to see what light the canto following II, ii can cast on its predecessor; the two cantos employ different characters and are not part of the same story, but their sequential juxtaposition makes and perhaps insists upon the comparison. What emerges from what Mr. Berger calls the "conspicuous irrelevance" of II,iii is an ideal of natural temperance that does indeed expand our awareness of the possibilities of virtue beyond anything that the homilies of Medina, Guyon, and the Palmer have allowed us to see. But Mr. Berger then goes on:

> Guyon identifies himself with Medina and sees her as embodying the conscious chivalric ideals he himself espouses; both feel it is their responsibility to

[6] Harry Berger, *The Allegorical Temper* (New Haven: Yale University Press, 1957), p. 159.

maintain justice and order in the world. But Belphoebe's nature also resembles Guyon's and reflects a
somewhat different light upon him: though she speaks
of honor and decorum and justice she herself is un-
encumbered by their problems. The unconscious character of her temperance is highlighted more clearly
than Medina's, and we are shown the innate self-
absorption underlying Guyon's social concern.

This in part only repeats the point made earlier, but
when Mr. Berger speaks of the "innate self-absorption
underlying Guyon's social concern" he is talking about
something he has mined from cantos far removed from
those in question—and all come later. It is difficult, even
for one looking for what Mr. Berger wants him to see,
to read the episode of Belphoebe and Bragadocchio and
see in it an illumination or reflection of Guyon's self-
absorption. This way of reading both reverses Spenser's
sequence and foreshortens it drastically; in effect, it im-
agines the sequence is not there.

The sequence, thus, is both extremely important and
difficult to remember, but this need not be a contradic-
tion. The sequence one attends to, given the length of
the poem, is a relatively local matter precisely because
the further we go on the more the earlier episodes become
misty. When the story moves along with one central character in a fairly tight sequence it is not difficult to remember three or four cantos. But when, as in the opening
cantos of Book IV, Spenser is constantly shifting his cast
of characters and leaving the scenery bare, it is hard
enough just to determine who is doing what to whom, to
say nothing of remembering what happened sixty or
seventy stanzas earlier. This difficulty is quite obviously
one calculated by Spenser and we do come to realize that
part of Spenser's "point" is that Paridell is here almost

indistinguishable from Blandamour and that both are much like Ferramont or Bruncheval. This varying of our sense of the sequence is one of Spenser's major techniques and when he is at his best the sequence is almost always rich and fascinating. For instance, III,v describes the healing of Timias by Belphoebe and his subsequent wounding by his love for her. The episode is "beautiful" according to C. S. Lewis, and most readers have agreed, yet lifted from the context provided by the sequence it would hardly seem so. But the previous canto is a series of laments for lost or unfound loves—Britomart's for Artegall, Cymoent's for Marinell, Arthur's for Florimell and Gloriana—and the resultant aura is one that seems to deny the possibility of any satisfactory human communication or love. After this canto even the silent and painful healing and wounding of Timias seems like a great deal, and it shines a ray of light in a dark world. After this episode comes the debate between Venus and Diana, a scene far more brightly and warmly lit than the one just before; we gradually are made ready, thus, for the Garden of Adonis, within whose grave joy we find no distinction made between human love and universal harmony: "But she her selfe, when ever that she will, Possesseth him, and of his sweetnesse takes her fill." The loneliness and despair of the human loves are not denied by the image of the Garden, but our sense of that loneliness is of course modified by it, just as, in turn, our sense of the Garden is modified by the simple and unabrupt return to "the world" in the following canto. It is one of the most brilliant sequences in the whole poem; deny it, pull any of its parts out of place, and the episode will seem quite different. What connects here is only sequence, there are no causal connections whatever among the episodes. It matters not at all in the "life" of

Belphoebe whether she sees Timias or Bragadocchio first, but it makes all the difference to the poem that each meeting is placed where it is.

One final example is perhaps most instructive of all. Thomas P. Roche, Jr., offers a fine and detailed account of Britomart's experience at the House of Busirane, after which he concludes:

> What then does this make of Busyrane? Is he not the abuse of marriage just as his house is the objectification of Amoret's fears of marriage? He is the abuse of marriage because his mask of Cupid presents an image of marriage as a sacrifice just as Busiris was a place of sacrifice. He is an abuse of marriage because the mind he possesses cannot distinguish between the act of marriage and adulterous love. He is an abuse of marriage because the falsity of his view of love can lead only to lust or death. His power is derived from the *abusion* of mind in distorting the image of love. The meaning he presents to the wedding guests is trivial, at the most, lust; the meaning he presents to Amoret is the sacrifice of personal integrity.[7]

This seems both excellent and unnecessarily wrong. Busirane is to Mr. Roche an abuse of marriage at the end of Book III because he is coming to these cantos via the descriptions of Busirane in IV,i. He has rearranged the events in the "life" of Amoret to put them in chronological order. He then interprets events in the light of sequentially later (though chronologically earlier) happenings. But no one, I think, coming on the House of Busirane after the episode of Malbecco would ever think as exclusively as Mr. Roche does of Busirane as an abuse

---

[7] *The Kindly Flame* (Princeton: Princeton University Press, 1964), p. 83.

of marriage. Nor need he do so. Mr. Roche's best sentence here can be easily rewritten to read: "He is an abuse of chaste love because the mind he possesses cannot distinguish between chastity and adulterous love." One needs to make clear what "chastity" means, and chastity perhaps does imply marriage to the extent that our image of chaste love in Book III is the married union of Britomart and Artegall. That is why the emphasis Mr. Roche makes on marriage by transposing the events is unnecessary; we can assume it to the extent that is really needed.

It is almost always in the interest of a conceptual distinction that critics have found it convenient implicitly to rearrange or foreshorten the poem's sequence; what is most obviously "there" as we read has thus been overlooked or underemphasized as though we were meant to read the poem in some conceptually clearer sequence than the poem's. Furthermore, the effort to find thematic and allegorical patterns and parallels tends to deny the fact that the conceptual scheme of things is something Spenser is really explaining to us all the time. The allegorical centers like the Garden of Adonis and the House of Holiness are in the poem, but the poem does not exist for their sake. What they crystallize at their best is something which is part of almost every stanza, part of the monotonous yet beautiful tone that keeps assuring us that Spenser knows, that he can clarify, that above all there is no hurry. Here, there, all along, what is most important is always most clear:

> *And comming to that fishers wandring bote,*
> *That went at will, withouten card or sayle,*
> *He therein saw that yrkesome sight, which smote*
> *Deepe indignation and compassion frayle*
> *Into his hart attonce: streight did he hayle*
> *The greedy villein from his hoped pray,*

Of which he now did very litle fayle,
And with his staffe, that drives his heard astray,
Him bett so sore, that life and sence did much dismay.

(III,viii,31)

This is Proteus rescuing Florimell from the fisherman, and while there is nothing particularly unusual about the stanza it shows us the way almost every stanza does what is most important to Spenser. Proteus sees the sight and the sight "smote" him with deep indignation. The metaphor is then stretched as not only indignation but compassion is "smote," and finally it is lost altogether when the compassion that the sight "smote" is "frayle." Here is that characteristically loose syntax that is the surest sign of an undramatic writer: "frayle" floats free of the verb which controls its noun just as the adverb floats freely in Keats' "Alone and palely loitering." Compassion is frail; the truth is true regardless of the particular situation. Yet there is reason for calling compassion frail at this point—the sight, Florimell, is frail; it is frail because it is not compassion but indignation which causes Proteus' first move, his beating of the fisherman; it is frail because compassion is thus a weak human feeling. After this comes the beating, and without warning "life" and "sence" appear on the scene to be "dismayed" because the fisherman is near death. We know why they come but we will never know where they "came from" or "go to." But we see that we are not alone, none of us, not even the lustful fisherman; life and sense hover here, compassion is frail, and these are shown to be not so much the facts of this situation as they are the facts of life. At every point Spenser is there to tell us of these facts. What Proteus, Florimell, or the fisherman know or apprehend is secondary at best, materials of the dramatic writer, important only if we need to stress that each of us sees the world differently.

We read on and on in *The Faerie Queene* not to find out what happens to a particular character but to follow Spenser's sequence, the evenness and unhurriedness of which is the mark of his assurance that he knows what life is like and that he can reveal the wellsprings of that life if we will but look. Faerie Land is a misty place because, in one sense, we are always lost in it. We have no bearings and nothing is ever tied down, nothing need be consistent. But at the same time we are never lost, there are no gaps, and we never feel the excitement and terror and suspense that the uncertainty of what will happen next forces upon us. For Spenser, to be uncertain is to be blind because an uncertain person accepts the consciously apprehended world as the whole truth. Were we to see Florimell and the fisherman in dramatic terms we would see them as uncertain; they would not and could not know that compassion frail smote Proteus' heart or that life and sense were dismayed. They are, like us, limited, tied to themselves. But Spenser insists, in this stanza and in the slowly unraveled sequence of stanzas, that what we see is but "seems" and that he knows what "is." Such is the solemn assurance of the undramatic writer. He knows we may become lost in the wandering wood and fall into mazy error, for such is the human condition. Life is wretchedness, Britomart tells Scudamour before the flames surrounding the House of Busirane. But the voice that knows this knows there is more. Spenser is the great priest of our uncertainty, hovering over us, quietly and effortlessly showing us that to be uncertain and lost is to be blind as well as human, and that it is possible to see. Every line he writes is there to show us we are not alone.

∾

But if we are not alone, what kind of world do we live in? The discussion thus far has focused attention on the kind of poem *The Faerie Queene* is and the problems of interpretation that most usually arise. But of the nature of Faerie Land, the stuff of the poem, the sense of life it conveys—what of these? If it is undramatic, Christian, and neo-Platonic, so too are other works of nothing like its scope or stature or particular feel. If the sequence is of supreme importance, then nothing less than close analysis of long stretches of the poem can convey an adequate sense of this. But before embarking upon such an analysis, some general points can be made.

Donald Davie once said of Shakespeare and Hopkins that there was no word in the language they might not use should the need arise. Spenser's vocabulary is by these standards limited, though of course it is very large. What we are perhaps most aware of are the repetitions, the apparently incessant use of a relatively small number of words. The Spenser concordance shows a handful of uses of some of his more famous archaisms and racy words almost swamped alongside lists of words that go on for a column or more—to pick words from only one section of the alphabet, we find more than fifty uses of "fayre," "good," "foul," "dear," "full," "force," "hand," "heaven," "gold," "glory," "great," "green," "ground." The adjectives are moral or meagerly descriptive, the nouns are simple objects in daily view, the verbs are simple and active. Above all, the vocabulary is monosyllabic. Much of this is the result of using adjectives as metrical and stanzaic fillers, and much too is the result of not working very hard to find the right word when an ordinary one is available. But this is far from the whole story. Spenser

is not really a poet of epithets or verbal formulas; what
we find instead is a host of words surrounding one repeated word and a word used apparently to signify one
fixed thing but actually used to illustrate different things
in different contexts. Thus, around an abstract noun
Spenser will use a constellation of related adjectives:
"sorrow" is "dolefull," "lamenting," "fowle," "secret,"
"thrilling," "pensive," "stupid," "long," and "huge," while
"passion" is "great," "stormie," "dredfull," "restlesse,"
"raging," "troublous," "franticke," "sharp," and, just once,
"piteous." The aim seems a suggested range of meanings and associations which will have a hidden but
finally telling effect on our sense of Spenser's feeling
about the quality conveyed by the noun. The common
nouns, however, seldom have such constellations, and
even when they do the appearances may be deceiving.
Day and night, light and dark—these do remain constant
and thereby attain the status of abstractions. But the
fountain of Diana's transformed nymph is "dull" and
"slow" while Chrysogonee bathes in a "fresh" fountain
far from all men's view and Archimago's fountain beside
his hermitage is "sacred" and flows from a "christall
streame." Gold is lavishly used in the furnishing of both
the House of Pride and the Temple of Venus. The things
of Faerie Land can be good, bad, or deceiving.

But more important is Spenser's way of charging almost everything, every action, every attribute with a kind
of moral valence. Look at what happens to "emptie" in
the description of Orgoglio and to "rude" in the description of Belphoebe:

> Brought forth this monstrous masse of earthly slyme,
> Puft up with emptie wynd, and fild with sinfull cryme.
>
> (I,vii,9)

> *In her rude heares sweet flowres themselves did lap,*
> *And flourishing fresh leaves and blossomes did enwrap.*
>
> (II,iii,30)

Here the words that might seem like filler words—"monstrous" and "earthly" and "sinfull" in the description of Orgoglio—really are a kind of lumber making the necessary scaffolding that will support and define "Puft up with emptie wynd," so that the moralizing epithets really exist to give moral valence to the words around them. No one readily recognizes this effect taking place as it happens, but slowly and silently the world of things is made to inhabit a land of profoundly moral weather, a land indeed of Faerie, made alive by the very words that often seem most dead, as in this simile about the dragon in Book I:

> *As burning Aetna from his boyling stew*
> *Doth belch out flames, and rockes in peeces broke,*
> *And ragged ribs of mountaines molten new,*
> *Enwrapt in coleblacke clowds and filthy smoke,*
> *That al the land with stench, and heven with hor-*
> *   ror choke.*
>
> (I,xi,44)

Here "filthy" and "horror" are the easy moralizing words, yet they also transform our sense of "boyling," "belch," "broke," and "molten," words held in moral suspension until the last two lines of the stanza.

In such a Faerie Land the potential density or complexity of feeling will be modified by the constant moral shadings; things rightly seen are seen morally, but the moral seeing is so constant and effortless that our final sense is not of "moral" as a means of strictly dividing good from evil, but of knowing the endless variety of things seen and ways of seeing open to the moral vision. Again, only prolonged analysis can reveal the enormous range of this variety, but even a brief look at two of the poem's great moments can help show Spenser's undramatic inclusiveness and his moral generosity towards his own imagination.

> What man so wise, what earthly witt so ware,
> As to discry the crafty cunning traine,
> By which Deceipt doth maske in visour faire,
> And cast her coulours died deepe in graine,
> To seeme like Truth, whose shape she well can faine,
> And fitting gestures to her purpose frame,
> The guiltlesse man with guile to entertaine?
> Great maistresse of her art was that false dame,
> The false Duessa, cloked with Fidessaes name.
>
> (I,vii,1)

At the heart of Book I this question illuminates all too clearly the plight of the Red Crosse Knight. The paynims and the monsters, the enemies that announce themselves as enemies, are relatively easy for the Knight, while the figures who tempt, waylay, and defeat him are all hidden in their evil, masters of their illusions "By which Deceipt doth maske in visour faire." (Incidentally, the moral valence given to "died deepe in graine" and especially to "fitting" are nice instances of the kind of work done by the surrounding flat moral tags.) Just before this opening to Canto vii Archimago, disguised as a pilgrim, has tried to crush Una by telling her the Red Crosse Knight is dead. Though he fails he follows close behind her as she leaves Satyrane to fight Sansloy. Then, just after this stanza, Spenser returns to the Knight who, having defeated Sansjoy and painfully left the dunghill of carcasses in the House of Pride, sits down by a fountain.

Weary, he removes his armor. His horse eats of the grass and he too "feedes," "upon the cooling shade." Duessa finds him and upbraids him a little for having left her in the House of Pride, but soon "they gan of solace treat," and together they "bathe in pleasaunce of the joyous shade." We need not note, particularly, an irony in that "joyous," for soon Spenser will show how deceitful, temporary, and disastrous that joy is. The shade of the tree protects a fountain that came into being because one of Diana's nymphs, just like the Red Crosse Knight, once when she was "quite tyr'd with heat," "Satt downe to rest in middest of the race." Diana, angry with the nymph's laxness, made the waters that flow from her "dull and slow" so that "all that drunke thereof did faint and feeble grow." What Spenser is doing here is merging the Red Crosse Knight with the landscape. First the Knight and his horse feed on the grass and shade, then he and Duessa bathe in it. Then he drinks of the nymph's waters, and of course "Eftsoones his manly forces gan to fayle":

> And mightie strong was turnd to feeble frayle:
> His chaunged powres at first them selves not felt,
> Till crudled cold his corage gan assayle,
> And chearefull blood in fayntnes chill did melt,
> Which, like a fever fit, through all his body swelt.
>
> (I,vii,6)

At first he does not feel what is happening, and then even when he does he does not realize its consequences. The cold of the waters chills the "chearefull blood" which is also his courage, and the transformed liquid swells through his body like a fever:

> *Yet goodly court he made still to his dame,*
> *Pourd out in loosnesse on the grassy grownd,*
> *Both carelesse of his health, and of his fame*
>
> (I,vii,7)

The wonderfully supple syntax here allows the second line, "Pourd out in loosnesse on the grassy grownd," to modify both the subject (he) and the object (his dame) in the first line. Thus both the Red Crosse Knight and Duessa become like the fountain, poured out, both being careless of his health and fame. As he becomes liquefied, as it were, he becomes feeble, faint, and uncaring, so hero, villainess, and landscape all dissolve into one.

Then "at the last he heard a dreadfull sownd," Orgoglio appears and quickly subdues the Knight. He is a giant, proud of his strength, boastful and arrogant, "Puft up with emptie wynd." He is about to kill the Red Crosse Knight when Duessa asks him to make the Knight his slave and her his mistress. Orgoglio agrees, the Red Crosse Knight is imprisoned, and both victor and vanquished are captured by Duessa. Orgoglio here is like the fountain, an external object that serves as a mirror for what the Knight has become. Careless, without his armor, the Knight drinks and becomes like the fountain. He is now "at one" with Duessa, they are poured out on the ground, so he meets Orgoglio, the very thing he has allowed himself to become; thus, both Knight and giant are ensnared. It is a marvelous spectacle of human degradation; by means of his allegorical figures, his Faerie landscape, and his freely inventive syntax Spenser does in less than a hundred and fifty lines what many novels have taken hundreds of pages to do less well. This way of working, using the external figures and landscape as mirrors, is, we slowly see, superbly appropriate for a book in which the enemies all really lie within and where the fatal vice is believing one has triumphed.

Early in Book I the Red Crosse Knight goes into the wandering wood and defeats the monster Error. If we were committed to a strict allegorical interpretation of events this would be puzzling because while "the Red Crosse Knight defeats Error" summarizes the plot, it does not state the meaning of the episode. Nor can we come much closer by making the statement read "Holiness defeats Error with the help of Truth"; the Red Crosse Knight does not defeat error in the abstract sense and he does not fight in a particularly holy way. But we can say that the Christian knight, by himself, because he is mortal, is liable to be "wrapt in Errours endlesse traine" and that, with the exhortation to "Add faith unto your force," he *can* defeat error—the monster or the human fact. The episode, thus, is an emblem of human possibility, a description of what can happen. Yet what is possible is of course not always what is; immediately after defeating Error the Red Crosse Knight "errs" in the hermitage of Archimago. In Canto vii carelessness with himself and neglect of his armor lead the Knight into the clutches of the proud and equally unheeding Orgoglio; this too is an emblem of human possibility. Of course theologically all sins are versions of pride, but this, we notice, is not the point stressed here; what is important is the way Spenser fills the landscape with those very qualities which the Red Crosse Knight cannot see are within him. The illusion evil is best at creating is the illusion that enemies are really external and visible.

Milton's famous pronouncement about Spenser in the *Areopagitica* is not really adequate to Spenser's sense of life in Book I. Undoubtedly Spenser could not praise a fugitive and cloistered virtue either, but neither was he the creator of Abdiel. In Book I struggle is necessary and constant but not, therefore, good and certainly not ennobling. The Red Crosse Knight is purified not in battle but in the House of Holiness. Milton's epic imagination was more challenged by godly struggle than by holiness, but Spenser casts a continual shadow across the whole idea of such struggle. Evil is disguised and deceitful and is therefore an illusion, but because we are liable to believe the illusion real, evil is constantly able to weaken its enemy.

The very idea that good can conquer evil is in Book I the most monstrous of illusions and is the one most certain to lead to self-destruction. Over and over the Red Crosse Knight wins only to lose. Being on the plain is debilitating because it puts the Knight where he cannot know what he sees "out there" is an image of himself. That is why the Giant Despair is the greatest of enemies, for he knows all this, he knows the appeal of rest and can sound to the weary ear so much like Contemplation. After a career of seeing triumph lead to error and degradation, the Red Crosse Knight by himself cannot distinguish between the two voices that assure him they know how heavily sin can weigh upon a sinner and how eager the sinner must be to be rid of himself. Thus we can see why Book I has more of a story than the other books and why its central figure is least the embodiment of the virtue he represents. We can perhaps see also why there is no need to describe the book as the education of its hero. The process of redemption is clear enough and the separate episodes do not so much form a causally connected narrative as they do a tapestry of emblems, the final emphasis of which is that there *is,* really, no education for the Red Crosse Knight because the presumption of such an education would be that one can learn to defeat evil and be holy once and for all. It is for this reason that Book I is stiffer, more stately and uncompromising than the books that follow. This is as it should be, of course, for its goal is only partly of this world and is not attainable on the plain or in the House of Holiness, or in the poem even, except as promise.

But having taken this position, Spenser is not committed to maintaining it or discarding it, and it is only in dimly analogous ways that the distinctive techniques of Book I appear again in the poem. The passage that is technically, morally, and emotionally at the furthest remove from it, to which we now turn, is not contradictory of it. It is simply another part of Faerie Land and, no matter how different it may seem from Book I, no one would ever doubt that it came from the same poem as the episode of Duessa and Orgoglio. As with the episode just discussed, we must watch the language closely to see it form and re-form our sense of the Faerie world. In I,vii, the action of the stanzas is "consistent" in that each stanza shows us a further stage in the degradation and capture of the Red Crosse Knight. In the meeting between Britomart and Artegall in IV,vi, the shifts are more sudden and wayward, designed not so much to fit into a single pattern as to provide a world so mercurial and wondrous in its variety that we can see much that the characters do not see without once losing sight of the marvelousness of what is possible for them.

As Canto vi opens, the situation is roughly as follows: Satyrane's tournament has grotesquely collapsed when the false Florimell cannot wear Florimell's girdle, Scudamour has been stupidly victimized by Ate and has wandered into the House of Care and out again, and Artegall sits sulking on the plain after his defeat at the tourna-

ment by a knight he does not know is Britomart. The
canto, thus, opens darkly:

> *What equall torment to the griefe of mind,*
> *And pyning anguish hid in gentle hart,*
> *That inly feeds it selfe with thoughts unkind,*
> *And nourisheth her owne consuming smart?*
>
> (IV,vi,1)

Here we see that the final result of the discord and fric-
tion promoted by Ate, Duessa, and the false Florimell is
self-contempt and self-hate, and that both Scudamour and
Artegall, as they sit on the plain, are thus crippled. Suddenly Britomart appears, the knights attack her, and just
as suddenly Spenser shifts his tone:

> *Who soone as she him saw approaching neare*
> *With so fell rage, her selfe she lightly gan*
> *To dight, to welcome him well as she can:*
> *But entertaind him in so rude a wise,*
> *That to the ground she smote both horse and man;*
> *Whence neither greatly hasted to arise,*
> *But on their common harmes together did devise.*
>
> (IV,vi,10)

There is no clear reason for Spenser suddenly to become
so playful; all we can do at the moment is to see that,
instead of a further descent into strife, he has given us
a lethally gay Britomart who "welcomes" and "entertains"
Scudamour by knocking him rudely from his horse.

Then Artegall tries his hand, and the focus shifts
again:

> *But to himselfe his felonous intent*
> *Returning, disappointed his desire,*

> *Whiles unawares his saddle he forwent,*
> *And found himselfe on ground in great amazement.*
>
> (IV,vi,11)

The playful Britomart has disappeared, to be replaced by the recoil of Artegall's "felonous intent." But the tone is the same—Artegall's desire is "disappointed" and, piquantly, he "forgoes" his saddle for the ground. But unlike Scudamour Artegall has only begun, and so as he attacks again, the tone shifts to something more somber —"And snatching forth his direfull deadly blade, Did leape to her"—and shifts once more as Artegall has his first "success":

> *So as they coursed here and there, it chaunst*
> *That, in her wheeling round, behind her crest*
> *So sorely he her strooke, that thence it glaunst*
> *Adowne her backe, the which it fairely blest*
> *From foule mischance . . .*
>
> (IV,vi,13)

There is a Britomart here, surely, but not really an Artegall; the "it" that glances down her back is an unnamed sword, and "it" does the "fair blessing" of destroying Britomart's horse, not because of Artegall but because of some "foule mischance." We can read "the which it fairely blest From foule mischance" as meaning "The blow from the sword was a blessing because it allows the two to fight subsequently on equal terms even though it was a misfortune because Artegall himself would never have struck her from behind." Or we can read it ironically: "This is the way savage knights like Artegall make love, by 'blessing' their ladies with blows down the back." There are more ways still to sort out the tones of such a pregnant phrase, but in any event, all readings ignore Britomart or Artegall or their visions or consciousnesses. The implicit assumption of these shifts is that there is no need to consult the characters. But this does not mean in the least that we can condescend to Britomart or Artegall, as the next stanza shows:

> *Like as the lightning brond from riven skie,*
> *Throwne out by angry Jove in his vengeance,*
> *With dreadfull force falles on some steeple hie;*
> *Which battring, downe it on the church doth glance,*
> *And teares it all with terrible mischance.*
>
> (IV,vi,14)

In four stanzas Artegall has been transformed from a buffoon who forgoes his saddle to a godlike avenger, and Britomart has changed from a Brynhild who laughingly entertains the men with blows to a defenseless steeple. In the episode in Book I discussed above, the changes were changes in the way we saw the Red Crosse Knight, but also changes in the Knight himself; here only Spenser's sense of immensely flexible possibilities is undergoing the metamorphoses.

Next Spenser backs off and lets the two grow large before our eyes, and for two stanzas they fight "Heaping huge strokes, as thicke as showre of hayle." But then Spenser once again steps in:

> *What yron courage ever could endure,*
> *To worke such outrage on so faire a creature?*
> *And in his madnesse thinke with hands impure*
> *To spoyle so goodly workmanship of nature,*
> *The Maker selfe resembling in her feature?*
>
> (IV,vi,17)

For a moment Spenser gives Artegall the heroic "yron courage" such a figure might presumably demand for itself, but then he expands his universe beyond such simple heroism. Britomart is not an opponent, such courage is irrelevant. She is, instead, an image of "The Maker selfe." But to see her *this* way is to say she is indeed a girl, and so he offers his final revelation:

> *The wicked stroke upon her helmet chaunst,*
> *And with the force which in it selfe it bore*
> *Her ventayle shard away, and thence forth glaunst*
> *Adowne in vaine, ne harm'd her any more.*

(IV,vi,19)

Artegall, we notice, has disappeared, and it is not the knight but the sword that strikes of its own volition and like a dumb animal stops when it rips away her helmet and, obediently, "ne harm'd her any more." Presumably what the sword "sees" to make it so responsive to the wonders of the universe is:

> *. . . her angels face, unseene afore,*
> *Like to the ruddie morne appeard in sight,*
> *Deawed with silver drops, through sweating sore,*
> *But somewhat redder then beseem'd aright,*
> *Through toylesome heate and labour of her weary*
> *   fight.*

(IV,vi,19)

This is done with lovely daring; in the final metamorphosis the "real" Britomart has both the face of an angel and a good deal of very human and very girlish sweat and flush. We need this, surely, this insistence that the "real" girl is what forces the sword to cease its mayhem. But we need more too, and to find it Spenser need shift no further than from the face that is "redder then beseem'd aright" to her hair that lights up Faerie

Land so brilliantly on each of its four appearances in the poem:

> *And round about the same, her yellow heare,*
> *Having through stirring loosd their wonted band,*
> *Like to a golden border did appeare,*
> *Framed in goldsmithes forge with cunning hand:*
> *Yet goldsmithes cunning could not understand*
> *To frame such subtile wire, so shinie cleare.*
>
> (IV,vi,20)

Britomart is a laughing knight, a steeple that receives the "fair blessing" of Artegall's Jove-like blows, a girl, an image of "The Maker selfe," a beauty beyond the power of art to make or to describe. The world is alive, immensely active, constantly in need of redefinition, and now, for the first time, Artegall begins to catch up with our sense of his world:

> *And as his hand he up againe did reare,*
> *Thinking to worke on her his utmost wracke,*
> *His powrelesse arme, benumbd with secret feare,*
> *From his revengefull purpose shronke abacke,*
> *And cruell sword out of his fingers slacke*
> *Fell downe to ground, as if the steele had sence,*
> *And felt some ruth, or sence his hand did lacke,*
> *Or both of them did thinke, obedience*
> *To doe to so divine a beauties excellence.*
>
> (IV,vi,21)

Surely only in a world so constantly changing and so filled with unseen powers can this cartoon-like conceit of the sword and the obedient hand seem anything but ludicrous. Spenser's magic is such that we can simultaneously be aware of the comedy of Artegall finally under-

standing what his sword learned before him, and of the
immensely mercurial world that makes us realize that all
responses are nigh inadequate. Here, though, as Artegall
looks on Britomart in amazement, sword, knight, and
author momentarily become one:

> And he himselfe long gazing thereupon,
> At last fell humbly downe upon his knee,
> And of his wonder made religion . . .
>
> (IV,vi,22)

The magnificent last line shows Artegall's reverence
for Britomart's beauty and Spenser's reverence for his
universe that has such possibilities in it. It also, perhaps,
reflects our awe of a poet who can move so effortlessly
and expressively through so many transformations without once losing track of them or himself. Artegall's response, thus, even though it is only dumb silence, is the
best one possible. Faced with a vision that none of his
own earlier roles as buffoon would enable him to understand, he changes once more and sees all we or Spenser
see. Earlier his arm was powerless, "benumbd with secret
feare," but now "trembling horrour did his sense assayle."
The horror does not tremble. Artegall sees he has assaulted a deity and so is attacked by horror and then
trembles. And well he might. He knows he does not understand, he wonders, and of his wondering incompre-
hension he makes a religion.

But Artegall's faith is powerless to hold Britomart still,
so she is transformed again:

> Nathelesse she, full of wrath for that late stroke,
> All that long while upheld her wrathfull hand,
> With fell intent on him to bene ywroke [to be
>   wrought]:

And looking sterne, still over him did stand,
Threatning to strike, unlesse he would withstand:
And bad him rise, or surely he should die.

(IV,vi,23)

With the last line here we are returned to the Britomart
who entertained Scudamour with blows; this command
is the gayest she ever gives. Without denying any comic
possibilities, Spenser continues to show that the gap
between "seems" (what the others see) and "is" (Britomart) is wondrous. First Scudamour, always willing to
commit himself lavishly, tries to outdo Artegall with his
fawning. Then Glauce reappears and, medieval character
that she is, seeks an end to both strife and celestial
visions. Artegall complies by removing his helmet and so
shows Britomart the face she had seen in her glass so
long before:

When Britomart with sharpe avizefull eye
Beheld the lovely face of Artegall,
Tempred with sternesse and stout majestie . . .

(IV,vi,26)

The face that had just been staring at her dumbly now
seems stern and majestic and lovely; like Artegall, Britomart does not "see" what is "there," and, like him, makes
of what she does see an act of faith:

Her hart did leape, and all her hart-strings tremble,
For sudden joy, and secret feare withall,
And all her vitall powres, with motion nimble,
To succour it, themselves gan there assemble . . .

(IV,vi,29)

Britomart also has her secret fear and is beset by powers
beyond her control, and so both Britomart and Artegall

make their most important gestures when they are filled
with surprise and wonder. We can see, if we like, that
Artegall is worshipping his mistress in standard courtly
fashion, but what Spenser is emphasizing here is the way
such worship is founded—not in convention, but in natural responses to one's beloved. Rather than stressing the
comedy of the scene, Spenser creates the comedy, and
instead of insisting on the limitations of the lovers that
give rise to the comedy, he stresses the possibility of acting upon these very limitations. What he knows is that
they enact their limits in a limitless world. At one moment Spenser and Artegall are together, implicitly praising their maker for showing them a larger world than
they had ever known. But Artegall is only a character,
locked in time, and so his moment passes, but instead of
working the comedy ironically against Artegall Spenser
really continues to do what he does throughout: reveal
the relation between men and an ordered universe. Given
his belief in such a universe it is natural rather than
conventional that Artegall made religion of his wonder.
Given this belief, furthermore, Spenser can easily show
that there is little that is mystical and much that is prag-
matic in his vision. To deny the wonderfulness of what
has happened by stressing only the confusion and the
blindness of his characters would be, for him, simply per-
verse. To give full play to the mysterious life of his universe he must show both the disarray of what his characters see and the shimmering possibilities for human
love that lie in the midst of the chaos.

So we have the stern and almost moody poet of the
liability of the Red Crosse Knight to fall into error, then
we have the mercurial wondering spirit of human possibility here in Book IV. What makes them part of the
same poem, what makes each in its way true and im-

portant, is simply the freedom that Spenser's undramatic
vision allows him. We note the inconsistencies of narrative and character, the absence of recognizable geography,
the shifts in mood, tone, and attitude, but these always
exist within the context of a sequence of stanzas that is
unobtrusively even and even-tempered. We see that
Spenser is undismayed and even uninterested in the same
kind of consistency sought for by a novelist. We see, for
instance, that at one moment false Florimell cannot wear
the true Florimell's girdle, and we know why that is so
because Spenser tells us. Then a book later false Florimell
is wearing the same girdle and Spenser does not worry
or even notice because he is now interested in something
quite different. The poem seems to move in an eternally
present tense with the sequence as Spenser's only struc-
tural device, so that the stanza directly in front of us and
those immediately preceding are, for us as we read, all
important. What happened a few thousand lines earlier
is as a long time ago—we know the poem feels as it always has felt and so need feel no strain if there seem to
be shifts in tone or inconsistencies in narrative.

But there is another way of explaining the difficulties
we may have with the Spenserian freedom. We have
often encountered moral universes, but usually they tend
to be restrictive, even claustrophobic. We may know we
"cannot do without morality," but we probably also side
with D. H. Lawrence when he attacks Tolstoi for denying Vronsky's masculinity for the sake of maintaining
his own restrictive social morality. So when we come on
a writer like Spenser who fills every stanza with "fayre"
and "foul" and shows us a world in which all actions are
charged with implicit praise or blame, we naturally are
tempted to think he is only old and that his ideas are
dead. Even the sternest and most reactionary among us

pauses before honoring temperance and a rigid idea of holiness. But to speak this way is to distort Spenser by stressing Spenser's ideas in a very narrow way; such remarks are usually made by those not really interested in reading the poem. In both episodes discussed above, Spenser's vision is clearly moral (compassionate and insistent in Book I, mercurial and wondering in Book IV) but because Spenser's task is to unfold what he knows to be true, not to promote any particular moral code. Of course Spenser has his narrownesses, and they are almost always the result of his occasional bland acceptance of the medieval allegorical tradition; Kirkrapine in Book I, and Medina and the House of Alma in Book II are at best deftly handled and rather mindless re-workings of the allegories of earlier poets. But this is not all *The Faerie Queene* or even very much of it, and only those interested in maintaining a particular social or religious ideal will stress these episodes in order to praise or attack Spenser. After all, interpreted narrowly any writer's ideas die very quickly, if they ever lived, and if we restricted ourselves to admiring only those authors whose ideas coincided with our own we would only doom ourselves to much rereading in a very small room and to ignoring the infinite riches outside.

No, the problems in reading *The Faerie Queene* are far different from those small difficulties we may have with Spenser's "ideas." Outside of the cumbersome fact of its great length, the major problem is seeing how a writer writes when he sees human life as his subject but not as the limit of his material. He is careless of much we implicitly admire—time, situation, and character seen dramatically—but we need not work up an argument about the parts of all of us that are undramatic in order to see that such carelessness is not beyond our understanding or our care. We need not be "born with a sympathy for such work" to see that great areas of our imaginations can be opened by a writer who feels a solemn joyousness in the fact that man is not the measure. When C. S. Lewis says of Spenser that to read him is to grow in mental health we may perhaps demur and add that C. S. Lewis says this because he believes what Spenser believes. But the freedom of the undramatic writer *is* a wonderful thing to behold in the service of one as inventive as Spenser. This inventiveness is of course a matter of artistic mastery, but the mastery is only superficially a matter of technique. It is the result of Spenser's knowledge and of its density and security combined with his constant sense of wonder. The freedom this gave him was profoundly absorbing to Spenser himself, and the absorption in turn meant he was never imaginatively in any hurry. His task was not to go anywhere, not to explore the edge of the unknown, but to embody and make imminent the endless aliveness of his received universe. Because it was so assuredly moral it had little need to be didactic. Faeric Land is a fact, not a doctrine.

There is a vast difference, then, between loving *The Faerie Queene* and being a Spenserian in the narrow sense, between being baffled, delighted, and bored with its endlessness and being convinced that one has to study oneself into the right frame of mind in order to read the poem at all. It takes study, of course, and even more it takes patience, but both study and patience are necessary only to see what is there rather than to transform oneself into a denizen of the mists. For the central fact about *The Faerie Queene* is not that it is old but that it is unique, and the real difficulty in reading it is simply reading it and not in making oneself an Elizabethan. To call the poem simple, it seems to me, is to be simple; to say it is not very well written is to fail to see what kind of writing it is; to move in quiet excitement with its movement is to be touched in a way that can never be quite eradicated or replaced. Spenser does not ennoble or elevate as later visionaries can do, he offers no sense of a personality to be met and felt. But the argument offered above and the few examples given of the ways of the poem are designed to begin to show that about the largeness and smallness of being human he makes all other poets seem a little confused. Perhaps more than anyone else, he makes us remember what we forgot we ever knew.

III 🐚 *Book III*

In "A Letter of the Authors" addressed to Raleigh and prefixed to Books I–III of *The Faerie Queene,* Spenser has this to say about Book III and the occasion which precipitated its events:

> The third day there came in a groome, who complained before the Faery Queene, that a vile enchaunter, called Busirane, had in hand a most faire lady, called Amoretta, whom he kept in most grievous torment, because she would not yield him the pleasure of her body. Whereupon Sir Scudamour, the lover of that lady, presently tooke on him that adventure. But being unable to performe it by reason of the hard enchauntments, after long sorrow, in the end met with Britomartis, who succoured him, and reskewed his love.

No one looking at Book III could possibly feel that this is an adequate summary of it or introduction to it, but no other summary would have done a great deal better. One way of stating the difference between it and the preceding books is to say that the outlines Spenser gives of them in the letter do correspond at least to one sense we have of them. Their form is not necessarily the form implied by their outlines, but in each a knight does set out to perform the adventure of a rescue and at the end of each the adventure is achieved. But Book III is not at all about the trials of Scudamour, and though it does end with Britomart's rescue of Amoret, that action has no narrative connection with much that precedes it.

But readers have always admired Book III, and most have felt few qualms about jettisoning the implied "structure" mentioned in the letter to Raleigh for the sake of the beauties they found in the twelve cantos themselves. It is true that the first two books have until quite recently received much the most attention, and it is probably true that the relative ease with which these books can be outlined has contributed to the sense of their superiority implied by this attention. In Book III all trace of "structure" in the novelistic or dramatic sense disappears and we are left with undramatic sequence as Spenser's only means of organizing his vision and his material. Though it borrows from Ariosto, furthermore, both in its method of interweaving the "stories" and in a number of its incidents, the book has little of Ariosto's sense of narrative suspense. There have, of course, been efforts to show that Book III is really as densely organized as Book I and Book II, just as there have been efforts to say that Spenser's form is really like Ariosto's. But though these efforts have failed, their authors show that they admire in Book III what everyone admires. We may not parcel out praise and blame to the characters with the Victorian nicety of Kate M. Warren, and we do not read after the strict allegorical manner of Frederick Padelford, but we can easily see what they saw. In broad terms everyone knows what Book III is all about—the morality of sexual love—and as long as we allow our terms to remain broad, we probably cannot add much in substance to the interpretations of earlier writers.

But, as we have seen, our terms need not remain broad, and the sequence that is Book III has never been carefully traced. Individual passages have been commented upon often, but if what was said in the previous chapter is correct, then commentary should try as much as possible not to pick out the best moments but to comment as we read, stanza by stanza. What we find, almost from the very beginning, is that the interpretational problems do not so much concern the virtue of chastity as its vices, and even more, their complexion when mixed. As befits a many-storied sequence, the lights cast by one event on those that follow are not always easy to see or define because the mixing is always taking place. More than in Books I and II, in Book III we are always wandering; Spenser has set no goal, no place of clarifying triumph; what happens next is only another and not always clearly related event. The form, to repeat, is the sequence.

❧

We begin Canto i with two different confusions, one apparently planned and the other almost certainly not. One of Spenser's neater instincts told him to provide bridges between the books, even when they are unconnected by any narrative link. The Red Crosse Knight and Archimago appear at the beginning of Book II, and

Spenser's point, simple though it is, is made neatly: the Red Crosse Knight is bequeathing Faerie Land to his successor on the basis of his own triumph at the end of Book I: "God guide thee, Guyon, well to end thy warke" (II,i,32). But the effort to get the Red Crosse Knight, Guyon, Arthur, Archimago, and Duessa into Book III is made with much more mixed results. Duessa is mentioned in the proem to the canto, but never appears; Archimago has a piquant and totally inexplicable one stanza appearance in Canto iv. In the opening stanza of the book Arthur and Guyon are described as leaving the House of Alma, but then, in order to account for the closing cantos of Book II, Spenser has Guyon send Acrasia off to Gloriana's court and then somehow catch up with Arthur on the plain. The meeting of Guyon and Britomart is not really more satisfactory, but at least it begins to show what Spenser is trying to do. Guyon and Arthur see a knight, Guyon rushes towards the knight, they clash, and Guyon finds himself on the ground. Guyon is furious, but Spenser tells us that something new has entered the poem; the spear is enchanted with "secret powre unseene." Guyon knows nothing of this, but the palmer does and warns him. Arthur adds that it was not the spear at all but Guyon's horse that caused the fall, and so Guyon and the knight, Britomart, are reconciled "Through goodly temperaunce and affection chaste." The palmer's temperance and Arthur's affection, we notice, are not at all abstract virtues, but worldly wisdom and social grace. Spenser expands on this in his apostrophe to the habits of ancient times which allowed for these virtues:

> O goodly usage of those antique tymes,
> In which the sword was servaunt unto right!

> When not for malice and contentious crymes,
> But all for prayse, and proofe of manly might,
> The martiall brood accustomed to fight:
> Then honour was the meed of victory,
> And yet the vanquished had no despight:
> Let later age that noble use envy,
> Vyle rancor to avoid, and cruel surquedry [arrogance].
>
> (III,i,13)

What is clumsy here is the gap between the praise of the "goodly usage of those antique tymes" and the behavior of Britomart and especially Guyon. Spenser is adapting an episode in Ariosto's *Orlando Furioso* and trying to turn a joke in the other poem into a solemn invocation here, but the evidence does not really square with the praise.

Still, this stanza and a number of other lines in the early part of the canto point up a somewhat different kind of confusion. The goals here are not specific like the destruction of the Bower of Bliss, but vague and chivalric. These knights fight "all for prayse, and proofe of manly might"; they "hunt for glory and renowmed prayse" and "to recover right for such as wrong did grieve." Praise and glory can be achieved in any one of many ways, virtue or triumph are not to be had in a particular time or place, but are, rather, achieved results of any kind of action. It is not, thus, going to be as easy as it was in Books I and II to accuse knights of truancy, nor is it going to be as simple to see where the sequence is going. The scenery is blank, knights appear and disappear, Guyon and Arthur could be any virtuous knights. Soon a lady races by followed by a lout, Arthur and Guyon run off after them. Then Britomart, now alone, comes on six knights attacking one. The stately movement of the opening of Book I and the emblematic qual-

ity of the first canto of Book II have been replaced by a
series of blurs, and only seldom in Book III will this
sense of blur and mist be dispelled.

In the next episodes in Castle Joyeous even more is
done to abolish some of the distinctions we could make
rather easily in the first two books. Although the distinctions are crude and immensely inadequate to our total
sense of the books, the differences between "good people"
and "bad people" are generally clear up to this point in
the poem. With each new character we meet, we come to
expect to be told on which side of the moral fence he or
she is, and the complications seldom arise from any ambiguity or ambivalence as to the moral nature of each
character, except for the Red Crosse Knight and Guyon
themselves. Duessa, Archimago, the paynim knights, Orgoglio, Huddibras, Furor, Mammon, Maleger—all the
evil characters are not evil in the same way or to the
same extent, but we know soon after we meet them that
all are indeed evil. Likewise Una, the lion, Arthur, the
residents of the House of Holiness, the palmer, Medina,
and Alma—they are good in many different ways, but
all are, as we read, easily classified as a kind of "good."
But in our first major encounter in Castle Joyeous we
have something different, the Venus and Adonis of the
tapestries:

> Then with what sleights and sweet allurements she
> Entyst the boy, as well that art she knew,
> And wooed him her paramoure to bee . . .

(III,i,35)

The pleasures here are sophisticated, graceful, and de-
lighting in secrecy: "Now leading him into a secret
shade," "She secretly would search each daintie lim," "So

did she steale his heedelesse hart away, And joyd his love
in secret unespyde." The morality of this is far from clear;
we know, especially after the Bower of Bliss, the ways in
which the love that leads to secret bondage is far from
the highest love, but Spenser levels no charge against it.
Rather, he only goes on to the next tapestries:

> She oft and oft adviz'd him to refraine
> From chase of greater beastes, whose brutish pryde
> Mote breede him scath unwares: but all in vaine;
> For who can shun the chance that dest'ny doth ordaine?
>
> Lo! where beyond he lyeth languishing,
> Deadly engored of a great wilde bore,
> And by his side the goddesse groveling . . .
>
> (III,i,37–38)

The wound is not the wages of sin, nor is it the result of
being wooed by Venus. It is, merely, Adonis' destiny.
Venus has been unable to hide him from his fate, and
nothing remains secret forever. There is no clear moral
"placing" of either Venus or Adonis.

Next we have Britomart's encounter with Malecasta,
and although here Spenser does let loose some moral
thunderbolts, they are not allowed to stand as permanent
definitions of Malecasta. First we have Malecasta's discovery of her love for Britomart, whom she does not
know is a woman:

> Whom when the lady saw so faire a wight,
> All ignorant of her contrary sex,
> (For shee her weend a fresh and lusty knight)
> Shee greatly gan enamoured to wex,
> And with vaine thoughts her falsed fancy vex:
> Her fickle hart conceived hasty fyre,
> Like sparkes of fire which fall in sclender flex,

> *That shortly brent into extreme desyre,*
> *And ransackt all her veines with passion entyre.*
> (III,i,47)

This is courtly passion, like Troilus' before the temple or
Romeo's at Capulet's ball. Here is Spenser's comment:

> *But as a cole to kindle fleshly flame,*
> *Giving the bridle to her wanton will,*
> *And treading under foote her honest name:*
> *Such love is hate, and such desire is shame.*
> (III,i,50)

Malecasta is clearly a victim of her fire; the moment she
"gan enamoured to wex," all the actions are suddenly
ones over which she has no control. Her veins are ran-
sacked, her honest name is trampled, and all she can do
is feel the shame of her desire.

When Malecasta begins to disclose her love to Britomart, the latter's response is both touching and woefully
inadequate and thus comic. Britomart, we are told, has
no trouble believing that Malecasta burns because Britomart herself knows "what paines doe loving harts per-
plexe." She has no sense of Malecasta's confusion about
her sex, the disclosure of which would end everything,
but is only full of fellow-feeling, and so is courteous
to Malecasta. Malecasta now tries to read Britomart's
feelings from her outward actions and miscalculates,
"esteemd That from like inward fire that outward smoke
had steemd." Thus Britomart gets into trouble because
she can understand Malecasta's passion and forgets everything else, and Malecasta gets into trouble because she
cannot understand Britomart's passion. If one were parcel-
ing out moral tags, presumably Malecasta would be "bad"
and Britomart "good," but of course both are better seen

as victims—Malecasta of her passion, Britomart of her situation. Indeed, when Spenser comes to the climax of the scene it is Malecasta he extends his sympathy to:

> *Now whenas all the world in silence deepe*
> *Yshrowded was, and every mortall wight*
> *Was drowned in the depth of deadly sleepe,*
> *Faire Malecasta, whose engrieved spright*
> *Could find no rest in such perplexed plight,*
> *Lightly arose out of her wearie bed,*
> *And, under the blacke vele of guilty night,*
> *Her with a scarlott mantle covered,*
> *That was with gold and ermines faire enveloped.*
>
> (III,i,59)

Malecasta is sinister, but she had no choice. The others go to "kindly rest," but her "engrieved spright" only makes her bed weary and she is driven to make love under the mantle of the guilty night. She lies down beside Britomart, who discovers her:

> *She lightly lept out of her filed bedd,*
> *And to her weapon ran, in minde to gride*
> *The loathed leachour. But the dame, halfe dedd*
> *Through suddein feare and ghastly drerihedd,*
> *Did shrieke alowd, that through the hous it rong . . .*
>
> (III,i,62)

Spenser has made quite clear that "filed bedd" and "loathed leachour" are Britomart's responses, not his own, and the image of Britomart leaping up to get her weapons to save her from a lady lets her in for the butt of the comedy just as the description of the terrified and half dead Malecasta keeps the sympathetic view of her. Malecasta, after all, is victim not just of her passion but of

Britomart's "sensitivity." The comedy is complete when
Britomart is wounded, and although Spenser says "yet
was the wound not deepe," Britomart responds wildly:
"Wherewith enrag'd, she fiercely at them flew." She
never does see the joke.

Of course we can turn the matter around and insist
that Britomart is only the victim of Malecasta's passion
and that Malecasta's love *is* hate. But this, while true, is
not the direction Spenser moves. For in order to "place"
Britomart here it is essential that we modify our usual
sense of praising and blaming "good" and "evil" qualities
and see, rather, the comic inadequacies of Britomart's
response, first to Malecasta's disclosure of her passion
and then to Malecasta's frightened and engrieved trip to Britomart's bed. Seeing this, we know not only that we are a
long way from any sense that Britomart "is" chastity, but
also that the wound and the fire that is love cannot be
handled with any firm or inflexible moral sense. It is a
fine opening canto, perhaps the best in the poem, and it
puts us into a world the likes of which we have not quite
seen before.

In Canto ii much of Britomart's experience is pointedly
a variation of Malecasta's in Canto i. Malecasta had dis-
closed her desire "With sighes, and sobs, and plaints,
and piteous griefe," and now Britomart responds to the
Red Crosse Knight's question about her reason for being
in Faerie Land:

> *Thereat she sighing softly, had no powre*
> *To speake a while, ne ready answere make,*
> *But with hart-thrilling throbs and bitter stowre,*
> *As if she had a fever fitt, did quake,*
> *And every daintie limbe with horrour shake . . .*
>
> (III,ii,5)

Like Malecasta she holds the "stowre" and fever inside, and so she lies to the Red Crosse Knight about her knowledge of Artegall. Of course there are differences: Malecasta is a queen who has built her castle around the assumption that the wound of love burns all, while Britomart is only a girl employing feeble stratagems. When she first saw Artegall in the glass given by Merlin to her father, she had no idea what had happened:

> But the false archer, which that arrow shot
> So slyly that she did not feele the wound,
> Did smyle full smoothly at her weetlesse wofull stound.
>
> (III,ii,26)

The archer is false even though the arrow, presumably, is one of "true" love. Cupid appeared once in the first canto as a kindler of lustful fires, and a few stanzas later Glauce speaks of "That blinded god, which hath ye blindly smit." The point seems to be that the wounding arrow and the resultant pain and poison are not what is good or chaste about love, and there is at least a suggestion that some other kind of love, one not initiated by Cupid, is imaginable. But it is not developed here; Britomart begins smiling, but quickly becomes sick and unable to sleep, a pathetic because innocent Malecasta:

> 'Sithens it hath infixed faster hold
> Within my bleeding bowells, and so sore
> Now ranckleth in this same fraile fleshly mould,
> That all mine entrailes flow with poisonous gore,
> And th' ulcer groweth daily more and more . . .'
>
> (III,ii,39)

By itself this might not be comic, but Spenser does not

leave it by itself, for the girl is complaining bewilderedly to her "knowing" nurse, who answers:

> *'Daughter,' said she, 'what need ye be dismayd,*
> *Or why make ye such monster of your minde?*
> *Of much more uncouth thing I was affrayd;*
> *Of filthy lust, contrary unto kinde . . .'*

(III,ii,40)

Britomart's bowels bleed, her entrails are poisoned, her ulcer grows, but Glauce is relieved that this is all very natural, not "contrary unto kinde." But then, Glauce is right, and this is only adolescent love-sickness, about which Spenser, certainly, is neither very embarrassed nor very moved. If this scene is not exactly comic as are the scenes between Juliet and her nurse or between Troilus and Pandarus, it certainly is like them in its enjoyment of the gaps between love's victims and love's would-be votaries. Spenser can even go so far as to offer little comic thrusts himself—the women go to church and pray "With great devotion, and with litle zele"—but of course his commitment to the homeliness of Britomart's pain and Glauce's remedies does not commit him to remaining in that vein.

Canto iii opens with an invocation that puts the matter in a quite different light:

> *Most sacred fyre, that burnest mightily*
> *In living brests, ykindled first above,*
> *Emongst th' eternall spheres and lamping sky,*
> *And thence pourd into men, which men call Love;*
> *Not that same which doth base affections move*
> *In brutish mindes, and filthy lust inflame,*
> *But that sweete fit that doth true beautie love,*
> *And choseth Vertue for his dearest dame,*

> *Whence spring all noble deedes and never dying*
> *fame.*
>
> (III,iii,1)

The imagery remains as it has throughout: the fire is
sacred but lust inflames. If we seek to know how to distinguish love from lust, Malecasta from Britomart, we
cannot look to the cause, for in both cases it is celestial
fire, nor to the effects on the lovers, for in both cases it
is pain and desire. We look instead at the results, the
actions taken. Malecasta, however much we see her as a
victim, does move from her passion to seek domination
over others. But from those "that doth true beautie love"
"spring all noble deedes and never dying fame." This is
not, or is not yet, Britomart, but of her love he can say
it makes

> . . . *her seeke an unknowne paramoure,*
> *From the worlds end, through many a bitter stowre:*
> *From whose two loynes thou afterwardes did rayse*
> *Most famous fruites of matrimoniall bowre,*
> *Which through the earth have spredd their living*
> *prayse,*
> *That Fame in tromp of gold eternally displayes.*
>
> (III,iii,3)

Here we are back on the hard high ground with which
Book III begins: the proof of virtue is fame. But fame
here is not, as it was for Guyon and Arthur and even
Britomart earlier, a knightly goal. It is, rather, the historical result of fruition, and so it is to Clio that Spenser
turns to demonstrate the virtue of Britomart and to take
the poem, at least for the moment, out of the realm of
comedy. As Merlin tells Britomart after Glauce has taken
the girl to his cave:

'Most noble virgin, that by fatall lore
Hast learn'd to love, let no whit thee dismay
The hard beginne that meetes thee in the dore,
And with sharpe fits thy tender hart oppresseth sore.

'For so must all things excellent begin,
And eke enrooted deepe must be that tree,
Whose big embodied braunches shall not lin,
Till they to hevens hight forth stretched bee.'

(III,iii,21–22)

Quite literally, by their fruits ye shall know them. Impossible as it must seem to Britomart, irrelevant as it must seem to her and many others, Spenser is insistent that it is only in the centuries' travail between Britomart and Elizabeth that the fruits of love are manifest. The priest of love is a prophet, and it is not in the meeting of lovers but in historical chronicling that we have our first clear view of the nature and possibilities of chaste love. Merlin takes the arrow of Cupid and, without denying that it is an arrow, turns it into a tree that must be "enrooted deepe" in Britomart. History is the growth of love.

Merlin's chronicle of kings between Ryence and Elizabeth takes up most of Canto iii. Most readers find this section and the similar one in Book II which gives Arthur's lineage among the dullest in the entire poem, and it is not possible to imagine anyone reading either chronicle carefully with enjoyment. But the passage here is not what anyone can call a failure. The verse moves along smoothly and Spenser is clearly in control of his vision. But one must share Spenser's antiquarian interests to find these stanzas really interesting beyond taking note of the ways Spenser has reworked history to give Artegall the place of Arthur and to skip over the period between

1066 and 1485. Some of Spenser's contemporaries obviously enjoyed this sort of thing, and it looks as though for Spenser an historical pageant was as fascinating as the procession of the Seven Deadly Sins in Book I or the Mask of Cupid later in Book III. We do not need to lament the fact that we do not share his fascination. But it should be said that Merlin's history is a tale of almost unbroken woe; though we do not learn of Britomart's response it is hard to see how it could have much cheered her up. Merlin insists that love, like truth, is the daughter of time, but he never even implies that fruitful generation is in itself good. He knows that Britomart's pain is the "hard beginne," he prophesies the eventual triumph of England in the reign of the "royall Virgin." Yet, after having arrived at Spenser's historical present:

> 'But yet the end is not.——' There Merlin stayd,
> As overcomen of the spirites powre,
> Or other ghastly spectacle dismayd,
> That secretly he saw, yet note discoure . . .

(III,iii,50)

Merlin is a magician, in control of all the world that Britomart or Glauce can comprehend, but he too can reach his limits and fall into a trance at the "ghastly spectacle" of the future. We move out, thus, for a moment, where neither Merlin nor Spenser can go; the note is ominous, perhaps, but because it is not given any highlights and because the poem moves smoothly on after Merlin recovers from his trance, we need not feel it comes to anything more than a lyric doubt of magician and author about the future. The present, here, is still very large.

The moment provides an opportunity to make a statement about early cantos in *The Faerie Queene*. We may not, as we read, think of each book as a unit, but because each book introduces us to a new set of characters, beginning to read each book gives a new sense of starting out. The subject—human life in the universe—does not change, but the emphasis does. This means that there must be something tentative about our reading in the early cantos of each book. We know we are being told all we need to know at every moment, but nonetheless, if Spenser's vision did not become clearer as we read, there would be no point in our going on. For instance, the first two books have their comic moments, but nothing on the scale of Britomart's scenes with Glauce. We may, coming on these, even after the comic moments in Canto i, feel we are not reading rightly if we find them amusing. Or, to take a smaller example, when Arthur and Guyon set off after Florimell in Canto i, Spenser pauses to praise the constant mind of Britomart, who does not give chase. It is fair to ask if this implies criticism of Arthur and Guyon. Or, in the instance with which we began, we may not know how much weight to give Merlin's trancing vision of the future beyond Elizabeth. We "see" what is "there," but often we may not know what to make of what is seen. Probably the only decent reply to this puzzlement is to say that if the matter is important Spenser will make it important by folding it into the fabric of his vision in what follows. As we read, if we cannot tell how strongly we are to interpret something, the best thing to do is to read on. If this is so, then the comic scenes do matter because there is a whole string of them, and each one makes it clearer that the fires, pains, and confusions of love do not, or do not yet, cause Spenser the alarm they seem to cause the characters themselves. At first sight we can say that loving and wanting *are* comic to the extent that they blind or debilitate. But, on the same score, Spenser's praise of Britomart does not imply strong criticism of Arthur or Guyon, and Merlin's trance is not as important as Merlin's whole "placing" of Britomart's predicament by means of historical vision.

Coming out on the other side of that vision we find that the comedy has been lost. Britomart sets out after the man whose face appeared in the glass and we return to Faerie Land where Britomart takes leave of the Red Crosse Knight. Nothing has happened to them since we left them in the middle of Canto ii, but the intervening flashback has happened to us. We now have a double vision of Britomart. On the one hand, because of Merlin's prophecy, she is a champion, a shining image, and so Spenser praises her:

> Yet these, and all that els had puissaunce,
> Cannot with noble Britomart compare,
> Aswell for glorie of great valiaunce,
> As for pure chastitie and vertue rare,
> That all her goodly deedes do well declare.
> Well worthie stock, from which the branches sprong
> That in late yeares so faire a blossome bare
> As thee, O Queene, the matter of my song,
> Whose lignage from this lady I derive along.
>
> (III,iv,3)

But that image of power, chastity, virtue, and historical triumph cannot change the "facts" of Britomart's condition, and so we come back to the lovesick girl, pathetic now and unprotected, as it were, by the confidence of Spenser's earlier comedy:

> And the deepe wound more deep engord her hart,
> That nought but death her dolour mote depart.
> So forth she rode without repose or rest,

Searching all lands and each remotest part,
Following the guydaunce of her blinded guest,
Till that to the seacoast at length she her addrest.

(III,iv,6)

Because to the girl Spenser's image of her glory is only a daydream, as she comes to the coast, guided by Cupid her "guest," it is not to knightly heroism or to the future that she turns, but to her sickness and loneliness:

'Huge sea of sorrow and tempestuous griefe,
Wherein my feeble barke is tossed long,
Far from the hoped haven of reliefe,
Why doe thy cruel billowes beat so strong . . .'

(III,iv,8)

But the answer that comes to her is Marinell, and what happens next is both heroic and destructive. Britomart is both immensely powerful and a pathetic victim, so that the double vision at the opening of the canto is easily and marvelously made one. As Marinell approaches:

Her dolour soone she ceast, and on her dight
Her helmet, to her courser mounting light:
Her former sorrow into suddein wrath,
Both coosen passions of distroubled spright,
Converting, forth she beates the dusty path:
Love and despight attonce her courage kindled hath.

(III,iv,12)

On the one hand Britomart is large and powerful as she converts her sorrow into wrath and beats the dusty path. On the other hand she is helpless as love and malice kindle "her" courage. We cannot say, then, who is responsible for what, exactly; Britomart acts, but love and

"despight" act on her. The result is courage, but of a kind
that can only act blindly:

> As when a foggy mist hath overcast
> The face of heven, and the cleare ayre engroste,
> The world in darkenes dwels, till that at last
> The watry southwinde, from the seabord coste
> Upblowing, doth disperse the vapour lo'ste,
> And poures it selfe forth in a stormy showre;
> So the fayre Britomart, having disclo'ste
> Her clowdy care into a wrathfull stowre,
> The mist of griefe dissolv'd did into vengeance
>   powre.
>
> (III,iv,13)

On the one hand Britomart is superb and large, able to
do as the heavens do. They feel the wind from the south
and "disperse the vapour lo'ste," and she sees Marinell
come and "disclo'ste Her clowdy care into a wrathfull
stowre." On the other hand her power is only the tool of
vengeance, and as she is a victim of love and malice, so
into such a victim she turns Marinell. It would be a
scary moment indeed were it not also so grand.

The knight threatens her and she pushes him aside:

> She shortly thus: 'Fly they, that need to fly;
> Wordes fearen babes: I meane not thee entreat
> To passe; but maugre thee will passe or dy:' . . .
>
> (III,iv,15)

The knight rushes at her, but of course he has no
chance; after two blows "He tombled on an heape, and
wallowd in his gore." She rides on, gazing at the gold
and pearls on the strond: "But them despised all, for all
was in her powre." That line indicates praise for Brito-

mart's being above earthly wealth, but it indicates also
the cruel, haughty air that Britomart's lost and frustrating
love has brought her to. The "all" that is in her power is
too much for her to bear. Thus, grand, heroic, lost, bitter, cruel, a victim but no longer a comic figure, Britomart leaves the poem and does not return until the ninth
canto.

At this point Spenser turns to Marinell and Cymoent.
Marinell is generically a type of the reluctant bachelor,
mythically and mythologically a type of Achilles and a
creature of the sea. But here, in Canto iv, what we see
is quite different. The parallels are all with Britomart;
both are victims, not of love but of destiny. As a character
he is almost impossible to assemble. He appears before
Britomart as a "mighty man at armes," an achiever of
"great adventures." But then his name and parentage
suggest something different: the famous earthly Dumarin
was his father, and his mother is Cymoent, daughter of
the sea god Nereus (thus the connection with Achilles);
his occupation is protector of the riches of the sea. All
this suggests a quasi-mythic relation with the sea. Then
again he has a third "role," his destiny as told to Cymoent
by Proteus, and this is only partly connected with the
other two. In the story he is wounded, on the one hand,
because of his and his mother's interpretation of Proteus'
prophecy. Cymoent warns him every day not to entertain
the love of women; he does not, and yet he falls. But on
the other hand he is wounded because Britomart, at the
moment he arrives, is ready to turn her sorrow into wrath.
Spenser is quite clear on this point: "But ah! who can
deceive his destiny, Or weene by warning to avoyd his
fate?" This is what Marinell is doing here, in Canto iv;
two knights collide, one deluded by a prophecy and the
other uncured by a prophecy. Destiny rules, as it ruled

Adonis, Malecasta, and Britomart, in incomprehensible and often ruthlessly careless ways. More than anything else, Marinell, Britomart, and Cymoent seem simply lost. Cymoent's lament after she discovers her wounded son, though on a different subject from Britomart's lament at the beginning of the canto, is equally the complaint of one buffeted by an unavoidable fate:

> 'O what availes it of immortall seed
> To beene ybredd and never borne to dye?'
>
> (III,iv,38)

This "says" almost the opposite of what Britomart says earlier, but the two sound very much alike:

> 'O! doe thy cruell wrath and spightfull wrong
> At length allay, and stint thy stormy stryfe,
> Which in these troubled bowels raignes and rageth
>   ryfe.'
>
> (III,iv,8)

To Britomart the pain of love leads to a plea for respite, while to Cymoent the pain of loss leads to a longing for an impossible death.

Marinell here, then, is one of a group of victims, and noting this fact shows how reading in sequence places a different emphasis from any derived from treating the story of Marinell as though the bits and pieces describing him over the course of three books were meant to be put together, as in a biography. Granted that there are hints here of a different, mythological function for Marinell, granted that he is tantalizing no matter how he is considered because he seems to demand a place in our sense of the poem larger than the few stanzas devoted to him here and there would suggest. We can grant this because

later he will belong with the obviously important Florimell. But that is later, and here Florimell has not been
introduced as part of his story. The Marinell that is important is the crowning figure of the end of Book IV,
not this further instance of a victim wandering and
desperate because tied to self. If we continue to read
the poem as it comes, Marinell's symbolic function will
become clear in due time. Certainly if we tried to find
the magnificent Marinell that "gins to spread his leafe
before the faire sunshine" in the cloudy knight on the
strond, we would be insisting on making the poem give
back what we gave to it.

A fit sequel to this episode is the splitting up of Guyon,
Timias, and Arthur, and Arthur's scene with the Night.
For here, as part of a story that has no narrative connection to those of either Britomart or Cymoent, we
encounter a third complaint against large and obdurate
forces. Arthur chases Florimell all day but loses sight
of her as night falls, and the prince lies down to sleep:
"The cold earth was his couch, the hard steele his
pillow":

> But gentle Sleepe envyde him any rest;
> In stead thereof sad sorow and disdaine
> Of his hard hap did vexe his noble brest,
> And thousand fancies bett his ydle brayne . . .
>
> (III,iv,54)

To a reader reading along and not finding anything
very remarkable, the first line above may not seem extraordinary, and certainly one can find many instances in
The Faerie Queene where Spenser has something happen
like what happens here. That sleep is gentle is hardly a
surprise, but that gentle sleep should envy perhaps is.
There is nothing gentle about what sleep is doing to

Arthur here: because it envies Arthur any rest, sorrow
and disdain vex his breast. The adjective has nothing to
do with the particular activity of the noun it modifies;
sleep is gentle, we know, because it refreshes, relaxes, and
quiets the sleeper, but here it is envious. The epithet is
not idly used, for the whole point is that sleep *would*
be gentle if it did not envy, but because it does, a
thousand fancies beat Arthur's brain and make it idle.
In such a world it is perfectly appropriate that Arthur
should blame the night for what has happened. There is
perhaps no more "point" to Arthur's complaint than there
is to Britomart's or Cymoent's, but that we are moving
on nonetheless becomes clear after the complaint is over:

> *Thus did the Prince that wearie night outweare*
> *In restlesse anguish and unquiet paine;*
> *And earely, ere the Morrow did upreare*
> *His deawy head out of the ocean maine,*
> *He up arose, as halfe in great disdaine,*
> *And clombe unto his steed. So forth he went,*
> *With heavy looke and lumpish pace, that plaine*
> *In him bewraid great grudge and maltalent:*
> *His steed eke seemd t'apply his steps to his intent.*
>
> (III,iv,61)

If we tried to paraphrase this stanza we might then
be able to see how much is here that we would have to
leave out. "The night passed and before dawn Arthur
arose, half disdainful but born down by the loss of
Florimell." We could, of course, give a closer paraphrase
than that. But it could hardly do justice in any event to
"Thus did the Prince that wearie night outweare." In
one sense it is Arthur who is weary and worn out; the
preceding stanzas of lament have shown this. But the
sentence says he wore out the night and made it weary,

and, if this seems like nonsense, we need look no further than three lines down to see that it is not. For Arthur "up arose, as halfe in great disdaine," and we see that though the night has worn out Arthur so that he proceeds "With heavy looke and lumpish pace," it is also true that he has worn out the night and is "halfe in great disdaine" of it. Arthur's lament becomes something both self-defeating because it wears him out and heroic because it wears out the night. The forces outside Arthur have done their worst, and they have done much. But in his lament he becomes heroic because he has done all that can be done to combat an eternal foe that brings with it "The dreary image of sad death." He has not won, for night will return and once again will hide "traiterous intent, Abhorred bloodshed, and vile felony." But night has not won either, for even before the morrow uprears his dewy head, Arthur too rises to seek and to rescue for another day. Of course Arthur need be aware of none of this; his stoic heroism implies no conscious effort.

So the three major episodes in Canto iv fall into sequential place and show us that what we are concerned with is not an ideal of chastity but with the attempts of mortals to act in a world far beyond their power to control or understand. It is a world without enemies; the struggles with paynim knights and with allegorical monsters of the first two books have been replaced by shadowy encounters that first are comic, then pathetic, and then, for a moment, heroic. Adonis and Malecasta are victims, so too in her totally comic way, is Glauce, and of course so are the figures that dominate this canto. In order to create this world Spenser could not use large and clearly allegorical pageants. Rather, the allegory, if it can be so called, takes place in the sudden appearance of sprite-like figures like "gentle Sleepe," or the "Love and despight" that kindled Britomart's courage, or "the blacke vele of guilty night" behind which Malecasta steals up on Britomart. The forces at work in the world to confuse and defeat are all named with abstractions, and in that sense they are like the obvious allegorical constructions, but all are hidden and unknown in their effects and actions.

Having paused thus long to summarize, we might make at least a preliminary comment on the qualities of Spenser's verse. Canto iv is a good one to discuss precisely because it contains none of the large set-pieces which are usually cited as evidence of Spenser's excellence as a poet. Anyone who has read this far in the poem knows that often Spenser does not "write very well," and F. W. Bateson once said that anyone who could cheerfully concede this could not really go on to claim greatness for *The Faerie Queene*.[1] Examples of sloppy writing are not hard to find:

> His uncouth shield and straunge armes her dismayd,
> Whose like in Faery Lond were seldom seene,
> That fast she from him fledd, no lesse afrayd
> Then of wilde beastes if she had chased beene . . .
>
> (III,iv,51)

This surely has more faults than it does lines. Each clause has a quite unnecessary and awkward inversion, and the last line—"Then of wilde beastes if she had chased beene"—borders on total incompetence. The diction has its share of clichés—"seldom seene," "fast . . . fledd," "wilde beastes"—and the rest is not far above that level. Perhaps the only fact worth noting is the "uncouth shield and straunge armes" that have taken the place of the "mightie shild" and "blade all burning bright" that Arthur has worn previously.

[1] *Essays in Criticism*, II (1953), 6–7.

Now compare these lines with some three stanzas earlier:

> So beene they three three sondry wayes ybent:
> But fayrest fortune to the Prince befell;
> Whose chaunce it was, that soone he did repent,
> To take that way in which that damozell
> Was fledd afore, affraid of him as feend of hell.
>
> (III,iv,47)

The first three lines here are also clogged with inversions that seem more the result of Spenser's need for a rhyme than of any desire to stress the verbs. The diction and meter are as flat and unremarkable as in the first passage. But here something is really happening. On the one hand, finding the path on which Florimell is flying is the Prince's "fayrest fortune"; on the other, having found the right way, "soone he did repent." Here "repent" seems to mean only "feel sad," and Arthur soon "repents" because Florimell will not stop at his call and soon night comes. Yet, of the three, Arthur has the "fayrest fortune." His is the luck of one who really is chasing beauty; Spenser is not praising Arthur here, but he is insisting that no matter what Arthur himself feels, his fortune is fairer than Guyon's or Timias'. There is something intrinsically fair in the chase regardless of the feelings it causes or the success of the venture. Spenser stands over Arthur and shows the values that Arthur himself, because of his consciousness of his sadness and failure, cannot know.

As phrases "fayrest fortune" and "soone he did repent" are as flat and uninteresting as any in the poem, but their juxtaposition makes them momentarily quite different. It is almost always by means of such effects that

Spenser makes himself clear, and what he makes clear is seldom a simple matter. Few readers would pay attention to this juxtaposition without forewarning, but what it seeks to express, after all, is what the whole canto has been saying in different ways, and it is by means of the gradual accumulation of such things that Spenser gains his "meaning." In a poem of such even tones, Spenser has no way of giving one stanza or episode much weight over another, and so he indicates almost silently what his world is like at the level of word and phrase in most of the stanzas. The slow movement of the poem is reflected in the slow movement of the stanzaic form, and any effort to break into the even flow would probably fail because the form would make it simply seem feverish or sluggish. Spenser's few apostrophes are allowed to dwindle away in their force before one stanza is over, and stand not as guideposts to the "meaning" but as momentary responses to the immediate situation. Whatever sense of Faerie Land we have, therefore, is almost bound to be the result of Spenser's successful working with the same materials that he in other places uses mechanically. We can see it as great or even good poetry only after we see what it is doing.

Perhaps we should not say that the verse is only functional, but what is good, measured by the standards of other long poems like *Paradise Lost* and *The Prelude,* is also usually flat. Both Milton's and Wordsworth's poems, though much shorter than *The Faerie Queene,* have many more memorable lines. But the fact that the poetry is often embarrassing to read aloud need not be a definitive judgment. We must read him slowly, not relaxing our sense of what good poetry should be, judging individual passages as well as the whole, but also trying to see if and how passages contribute to the whole. This is why our best terms of praise for his poetry often are "accurate" and "precise." When he is good he is simply being very clear about mysterious matters; he is precise in showing us what Arthur does and does not know, and so, in one more way, he is being precise about Faerie Land. The effect has to be cumulative because there is no other way; no single passage can give the same brooding and wondering quality that long stretches and the whole poem give.

So, as a preliminary judgment, let us say that Canto iv has no great things in it, nothing that would seem remarkable to anyone who has not read at least the first three cantos of Book III. We will come later to passages more clearly great than anything here, but we cannot read the poem just for these because they, like everything else, take on their particular coloration from what precedes them. In coming to terms with the more ordinary stuff of the poem we face the major difficulties most unsympathetic readers have, and for now we can say that for most of the poem Spenser claims no more for his verse than that it does its job, and that its job is to show the bases of his certainty about a world in which the characters may be lost but in which Spenser knows what life really is. What life "really is," furthermore, is only tangentially related to the large abstract nouns like "Chastity" which nominally outline his poem. Here life "really is" being lost or being made a victim, finding the path between self and committed goals beset with obscurities and obstacles. As yet in the poem no one has been able to move outside himself and toward the goal without an act of violence.

In Canto v more is possible. At the beginning the dwarf Dony appears, and we have, after a canto of laments and unseen encounters, a conversation. Dony identifies the fleeting maid as Florimell and Marinell as her love. Here Marinell's commitment against women is seen as something more purposeful than it did a canto earlier, for here he is refusing a particular girl and not, as before, simply being unaware of the un-knowable fact that Britomart is a girl. Arthur vows never to forsake Dony or the chase for Florimell, thinks for a moment of his squire Timias, and suddenly Spenser is focusing on Timias and his fight with the brothers of the forester who had been (but is no longer) chasing Florimell. The battle is rather standard, but at its con-clusion we have moved another step towards a new sense of possibility:

> So mischief fel upon the meaners crowne;
> They three be dead with shame, the squire lives
>   with renowne.

> (III,v,25)

The "shame" and the "renowne" are not really public, and are only values intrinsic to the battle itself, but Timias' "renowne" does indeed move us into a social world. The first to "know" Timias' bravery is Spenser himself:

> Now God thee keepe, thou gentlest squire alive,
> Els shall thy loving lord thee see no more,
> But both of comfort him thou shalt deprive,
> And eke thy selfe of honor, which thou didst
>   atchive.

> (III,v,26)

Spenser breaks in so seldom that when he does, even mildly as here, the effect insists that a moment not pass unnoticed. What we need to be told here, simply, is that

Timias, filled though he has been with wrath and vengeance, is nonetheless the "gentlest squire alive," one
capable of comforting his long departed lord simply by
staying alive. On the one hand the victim has become
more frail than Arthur or Britomart were earlier, but on
the other hand frailty is itself a kind of pathetic virtue,
so that living itself becomes a source of honor.

For one in such condition Providence extends relief, and the woods suddenly become those in which
Belphoebe hunts:

> Shortly she came whereas that woefull squire,
> With blood deformed, lay in deadly swownd:
> In whose faire eyes, like lamps of quenched fire,
> The christall humor stood congealed rownd;
> His locks, like faded leaves fallen to grownd,
> Knotted with blood in bounches rudely ran;
> And his sweete lips, on which before that stownd
> The bud of youth to blossome faire began,
> Spoild of their rosy red, were woxen pale and wan.
>
> (III,v,29)

There has been nothing quite like this earlier in Book III.
The victims Malecasta, Britomart, Marinell, Cymoent,
and Arthur, have been simply pale, poisoned, disagree-
able, complaining. Here we are not told that he "wallowd in his gore," but that the blood knotted his hair
into bunches of falling leaves, not only that his lips were
pale, but that they had had on them the bud of blossom-
ing youth. The victim is seen; providentially, Timias is
not alone. Cymoent presumes Marinell is dead and
laments, but Belphoebe is filled with soft passion and,
in a beautiful locution, "She cast to comfort him with
busy paine." The huntress feels "the point of pitty" and,
pained herself, makes busy to comfort him. Given the

lonely pain that has been modified hitherto only by the
helpless ministrations of Glauce and the "irrelevant"
vision of Merlin, this is a moment of great achievement,
and Spenser celebrates it quietly:

> *His double folded necke she reard upright,*
> *And rubd his temples and each trembling vaine;*
> *His mayled haberjeon she did undight,*
> *And from his head his heavy burganet did light.*
>
> (III,v,31)

The wound cannot be simply healed, but the burden can
be lightened; she dresses his wound and slowly he regains
consciousness:

> *He up gan lifte toward the azure skies,*
> *From whence descend all hopelesse remedies:*
> *Therewith he sigh'd, and turning him aside,*
> *The goodly maide ful of divinities*
> *And gifts of heavenly grace he by him spide,*
> *Her bow and gilden quiver lying him beside.*
>
> (III,v,34)

Because the gift of nursing is divine, Timias makes the
mistake made by many readers and assumes that what he
sees is also divine:

> *'Mercy! deare Lord,' said he, 'what grace is this,*
> *That thou hast shewed to me, sinfull wight,*
> *To send thine angell from her bowre of blis,*
> *To comfort me in my distressed plight?'*
>
> (III,v,35)

We know already that "Providence" "doth for wretched
mens reliefe make way," but it is no angel who gives the
relief:

> *Thereat she blushing said: 'Ah! gentle squire,*
> *Nor goddesse I, nor angell, but the mayd*
> *And daughter of a woody nymphe, desire*
> *No service but thy safety and ayd;*
> *Which if thou gaine, I shalbe well apayd.*
> *Wee mortall wights, whose lives and fortunes bee*
> *To commun accidents stil open layd,*
> *Are bownd with commun bond of fraïltee,*
> *To succor wretched wights, whom we captived see.'*
>
> (III,v,36)

It does not matter at all that Belphoebe, in one sense,
does not know who she is. The lady here is only
analogous to the goddess that confronts Trompart in
Book II, and were she in fact divine that poignancy
would be dissipated. Here we see the "commun bond."
Belphoebe is "like" the Belphoebe of Book II, "like"
Queen Elizabeth, even "like" a personified image of
virginal chastity. But here she is a ministering maid as-
serting the need of mortals to give succor and to stop
the victim from being "captive"—and in the context we
have here, "captive" means only "alone." Over and over
in the succeeding stanzas it is not chastity or grace or
regality that Spenser shows us, but human tenderness:

> *Where when they saw that goodly boy, with blood*
> *Defowled, and their lady dresse his wownd,*
> *They wondred much, and shortly understood*
> *How him in deadly case theyr lady fownd,*
> *And reskewed out of the heavy stownd.*
>
> (III,v,38)

But we do not escape the pain, for if the common bond
of frailty can be renewed, so too can the pain of love:

> O foolish physick, and unfruitfull paine,
> That heales up one and makes another wound!
> She his hurt thigh to him recurd againe
> But hurt his hart, the which before was sound . . .
>
> (III,v,42)

At this point the scene ends and Spenser shows us
two emblems of human fidelity, one shining and the other
painful, as salves and alternatives to the lovesickness
and frailty that are so clearly the common lot. The scene
ends because the two emblems are not compatible in the
narrative. First we have Timias' response to his wounding, the lyric choice to love his saviour silently and
fatally:

> 'What can I lesse doe, then her love therefore,
> Sith I her dew reward cannot restore?
> Dye rather, dye, and dying doe her serve,
> Dying her serve, and living her adore . . .'
>
> (III,v,46)

Such resolution does not in the least diminish the poison
or the pain of impossible love ("Yet still he wasted, as
the snow congeald"), but it does turn the plaintive loneliness of Britomart, Cymoent, and Arthur into a kind of
heroic virtue. Britomart asks that the pain cease because
she seeks to avoid the implications of what has happened
to her. But Timias accepts his fate and transforms the
pain and the dying into a living service to his love.

Spenser then says that Belphoebe knows nothing of
Timias' vow. When he adds that she "did envy" Timias
the "soveraine salve" of her love, Spenser dissolves the
narrative in order to praise virginity; she can hardly
begrudge Timias what she does not even know he wants.

But he has not dissolved the slowly forming bonds of the terms he has been using. The cordials Belphoebe used to heal Timias' wounds were herbs, panachaea, and polygony. When Timias is rescued he is laid in a glade of myrtle and laurel, and his wound is dressed in salves. As the thigh heals the heart is wounded, but the cordials and salves are there too, and "sweet." Here Spenser makes Belphoebe's gift of love, which she denies him, something that does not wound or burn: "that soveraine salve." But right in this stanza Spenser begins to move away from the immediate situation:

> But that sweet cordiall, which can restore
> A love-sick hart, she did to him envy;
> To him, and to all th' unworthy world forlore,
> She did envy that soveraine salve, in secret store.
>
> (III,v,50)

That the worthy Timias should suddenly be part of an "unworthy world" is not and cannot be a slight to him; the clause is there to define Belphoebe's virginity. It is not a grand or triumphant thing, not an asserted or militant chastity, nor is it virginity achieved by simple, prudent avoidance of the dart of love. Belphoebe's chastity is natural, and Spenser beautifully transforms her into an emblematic flower:

> That daintie rose, the daughter of her morne,
> More deare then life she tendered, whose flowre
> The girlond of her honour did adorne:
> Ne suffred she the middayes scorching powre,
> Ne the sharp northerne wind thereon to showre,
> But lapped up her silken leaves most chayre,
> When so the froward skye began to lowre:

But soone as calmed was the christall ayre,
She did it fayre dispred, and let to florish fayre.

(III,v,51)

At the beginning of the stanza Belphoebe and the rose
are separate—"More deare then life she tendered"—but
then Belphoebe assumes the powers of nature over the
rose, folding it against sun and wind, spreading it in "the
christall ayre." There is nothing coy about lady or flower,
nothing anatomical about the images, yet what is conveyed is a sense that what the rose does is a sexual
activity natural to it. The rose, the daughter of Belphoebe's morn, must be nourished, nurtured, cherished,
and if it is, we learn in the next stanza, it "beareth fruit
of honour and all chast desyre":

Fayre ympes of beautie, whose bright shining beames
Adorne the world with like to heavenly light,
And to your willes both royalties and reames
Subdew, through conquest of your wondrous might,
With this fayre flowre your goodly girlonds dight
Of chastity and vertue virginall,
That shall embellish more your beautie bright,
And crowne your heades with heavenly coronall,
Such as the angels weare before Gods tribunall.

(III,v,53)

Strictly speaking this is incompatible with all that
has preceded. Here women are not victims of a vision of
love like Britomart, or of lustful men like Florimell, but
are subduers of the masters of the world. It is thus imagined possible to live above what had been the human
lot—crowned by heaven, an angel before God's tribunal.
Just as the meeting of Timias and Belphoebe celebrates

the acknowledgment of frailty, so this emblematic rendering of Belphoebe celebrates a natural possibility above
such frailty. Mortals can wear their flesh like garlands
as much as they can allow their flesh to victimize them
with pain and shame. Of course this wearing is not
possible or desirable for all—that goes without saying.
Of course there is our by now distant emblem of the
fruitful love of Britomart and Artegall which had as its
key verb not "embellish," but "branch." But that was
prophecy and this is human possibility so rare and lovely
that it transforms Timias' pain into heroic stoicism and
itself touches the divine. We are indeed ready for the
splendors of the next canto.

Having moved from the aimless and destructive "meet-
ings" in the fourth canto to the painful but moving
meeting of Timias and Belphoebe, having then moved
from the mortal Belphoebe to a quasi-divine image of her
virtue, Spenser makes the next step—into the mythic—
easily. Here is the story of the conception of Marinell
in Canto iv:

> The famous Dumarin; who on a day
> Finding the nymph a sleepe in secret wheare,
> As he by chaunce did wander that same way,
> Was taken with her love, and by her closely lay.
>
> (III,iv,19)

It is difficult to imagine anything less joyous: Cymoent
lay asleep, Dumarin happened by, he lay with her. But
here, at the beginning of Canto vi, is another nymph
lying asleep, this time Chrysogonee:

> Upon the grassy ground her selfe she layd
> To sleepe, the whiles a gentle slombring swowne
> Upon her fell all naked bare displayd:

> *The sunbeames bright upon her body playd,*
> *Being through former bathing mollifide,*
> *And pierst into her wombe, where they embayd*
> *With so sweet sence and secret power unspide,*
> *That in her pregnant flesh they shortly fructifide.*
>
> (III,vi,7)

We can see from this both how far we have come and
how completely the place an event comes in the poem
dictates Spenser's rendering of it. In each tale a sleeping
nymph, but in one the meeting resembles that of Britomart and Marinell, while in the other we meet "Great
father he of generation."

We then move into the meeting of Venus and Diana
by means of a sort of review of Book III thus far. As
Venus seeks Cupid who "wandred in the world in
straunge aray," she looks first in places like Castle
Joyeous:

> *Ladies and lordes she every where mote heare*
> *Complayning, how with his empoysned shot*
> *Their wofull harts he wounded had whyleare . . .*
>
> (III,vi,13)

Then she moves into the haunts of the forester and his
brothers:

> *Then in the countrey she abroad him sought,*
> *And in the rurall cottages inquir'd,*
> *Where also many plaintes to her were brought,*
> *How he their heedelesse harts with love had fir'd . . .*
>
> (III,vi,15)

Finally she comes into the forests of Belphoebe's mythic
counterpart Diana, whom she meets accidentally:

> *She [Diana], having hong upon a bough on high*
> *Her bow and painted quiver, had unlaste*
> *Her silver buskins from her nimble thigh,*
> *And her lanck loynes ungirt, and brests unbraste,*
> *After her heat the breathing cold to taste;*
> *Her golden lockes, that late in tresses bright*
> *Embreaded were for hindring of her haste,*
> *Now loose about her shoulders hong undight,*
> *And were with sweet ambrosia all besprinckled*
>   *light.*

(III,vi,18)

This is very close to Ovid's description of Diana as seen by Acteon, and that story of accidental meeting and violent punishment might well have found a convenient place earlier in Book III. But here Spenser is interested in something different, in moving from Belphoebe to Diana. For a mortal girl virginity may be an embellishment, but for a goddess something more active is needed. Yet a long image of a virgin goddess like the description of Belphoebe in Book II would only have the effect of making Venus seem a vulgar intruder on something she does not understand, as Trompart is in Book II. But here virginity cannot qualify as the supreme virtue. So Spenser treats Diana physically and sensually, as a beautiful woman. Her modesty on discovering Venus behind her back is neither divine rebuke nor girlish affront, but lady-like dignity. Thus, when she has gathered her clothes and her nymphs around her, "Goodly she gan faire Cytherea greet."

Venus says she is looking for Cupid, and Diana answers scornfully that it must be terrible to be without "so good ayd To your disports." Venus replies that both goddesses have their place, Diana's in the woods and hers "In beds, in bowres, in banckets, and in feasts." She adds that she is afraid Cupid may have disguised himself as one of Diana's nymphs to "turne his arrowes to their exercize." Diana's reply is both angry and explicit: "Ne lend we leisure to his idle toy." Then Venus, seeing Diana's anger, "gan relent What shee had said," and speaks so softly that Diana is pleased and relents too by offering to send her damsels through the woods on the hunt for Cupid.

C. S. Lewis has called this scene a medieval *débat*, and adds that the reconciliation is possible here because Cupid is separated from Venus.[2] It is in the form of a *débat*, certainly, but as such it is very inconclusive because neither puts forward more than little arguments. It may be true that each goddess has her place, but when Venus says Cupid may have gotten out of his place by disguising himself as a nymph she means his place, like hers, is in beds, bowers, and feasts, and she has just been trying to extract him from these. Diana's answer is not really an answer but a simple denial and a threat—he is not here, and if he comes, "Ile clip his wanton wings, that he no more shall flye." But if as an argument it is all flimsy, as a scene it is remarkable. Despite their natural antagonism the two have a genuine conversation; one speaks and the other answers, communication and finally reconciliation are possible. If we think back to Malecasta's wooing of Britomart and Britomart's efforts to extricate herself, to Glauce's assurances that everything will be all right when nothing is right, to the brutal meeting on the strond, to the laments of Cymoent and Arthur, or to the healing and wounding of Timias, we will see that what is really goddess-like about the scene is simply its successful *human* exchange: politeness,

[3] *The Allegory of Love* (Oxford: Oxford University Press, 1936), p. 342.

respect for the feelings of the other, an ability to calculate those feelings and to act successfully upon those calculations. It is a magnificent shift, this, and it shows us clearly what we have known implicitly all along: that love is two becoming one by means of a graceful acknowledgment of twoness. Deeper things have been at work as well, and these we will face fully in the Garden of Adonis, but this more strictly human point about love is needed too, for without it the cosmic principles of generation would be merely cosmic. Spenser has slowly led us up to the mythic confrontation only to make his mythic figures grand and civilized women. The method, of course, denies all sense of levels, of strict distinctions between the human and divine, but, equally "of course," that is the point: the divine achievement of human love, the human achievement of divine love.

Only now are we ready for the Garden of Adonis, for with the finding of Belphoebe and Amoret we are really done with Belphoebe, at least for a long time. She has had her bower and she has shown that virginity is not in the least cold. Other possibilities than virginity must exist and Spenser must emphasize them, but still, Belphoebe's lifting of Timias' head does offer us our first real glimpse of achieved human love and her emblematic transformation into the natural goddess of the rose does offer us our first sense that mortals need not wait for history to achieve sexual fullness. If these episodes come before the description of the Garden, they must not be seen as a theoretical prelude to them, sexual purity before sexual union. Rather, they come where they do because Spenser can show in them possibilities not achieved earlier, and these can, as well, lead easily into the scene between Venus and Diana. Spenser is educating us, not creating a hierarchy.

Arguments about the Garden have tended to assume that we should try as hard as possible to make it all fit together with some kind of philosophical coherence. When these twenty-five stanzas are lifted and considered as a kind of separate whole, it is difficult not to make this assumption. It is a set piece, surely, but not therefore detachable from the sequence we have been following. Denis Saurat was able some time ago to suggest an alternative way of looking at these stanzas:

> The fact is that, in reality, philosophy does not come in here. We have before us a piece which is, in the main, lyrical. The poet wishes to express his feeling about nature's fruitfulness, a fruitfulness connected with the changes of nature; this marvelous fruitfulness is only the everlasting change of one and the same substance. . . . And there is the very deep feeling that nature is an animate thing, fruitful, sensual, and, unhappily for our feelings, eternally changing.[3]

M. Saurat arrived at these conclusions by finding it absurd as logical exposition, and Brents Stirling later showed that what M. Saurat considered absurd is not always so. Still, this statement can hardly be bettered. As we move through the Garden we become increasingly aware of the human representations of forms and substances, starting with elemental states and proceeding through Venus and Adonis to the maid Amoret:

> *Infinite shapes of creatures there are bred,*
> *And uncouth formes, which none yet ever knew;*
> *And every sort is in a sondry bed*
> *Sett by it selfe, and ranckt in comely rew:*
> *Some fitt for reasonable sowles t'indew,*

---

[3] *Literature and Occult Tradition,* cited in *Variorum Edition,* III, 345.

Some made for beasts, some made for birds to weare,
And all the fruitfull spawne of fishes hew
In endlesse rancks along enraunged were,
That seemd the ocean could not containe them there.

(III,vi,35)

The paradoxes pile up; the shapes and forms are "infinite," "uncouth," and placed in "sondry bed," yet they are also "ranckt in comely rew" and "enraunged," so the process is both "natural" in the sense of being wild and beyond order and "natural" in the sense of yielding orders, ranks, and beauty. The process is so wild and amorphous that no mind can discern its principles, yet also so orderly that the magnificent hierarchy of fishes, beasts, and reasonable souls is the result. Nature is mysterious, larger than human imagination and prior to it, yet also beautiful and orderly in ways we can all feel and see:

Daily they grow, and daily forth are sent
Into the world, it to replenish more;
Yet is the stocke not lessened nor spent,
But still remaines in everlasting store,
As it at first created was of yore:
For in the wide wombe of the world there lyes,
In hatefull darknes and in deepe horrore,
An huge eternal chaos, which supplyes
The substaunces of Natures fruitfull progenyes.

(III,vi,36)

The processes conform to an unimaginable precision whereby the stock is always the same so that what enters the world is always and exactly replenished. Yet all this is seen as the natural result of a chaos of primal darkness and horror. The myth forces us simultaneously to hold in focus an image of nature beginning in a horrifying chaos and an image of "fruitfull progenyes." Chaos,

on a scale far larger but in quite the same way as we
have seen from the beginning of Book III, is both awful
and necessary.

Having established his myth, Spenser proceeds to move
back and forth over our feelings about this process:

> *The substaunce is not chaungd nor altered,*
> *But th' only forme and outward fashion;*
> *For every substaunce is conditioned*
> *To chaunge her hew, and sondry formes to don,*
> *Meet for her temper and complexion:*
> *For formes are variable, and decay*
> *By course of kinde and by occasion;*
> *And that faire flowre of beautie fades away,*
> *As doth the lilly fresh before the sunny ray.*
>
> (III,vi,38)

We have come to accept the cosmic processes as con-
trolling the endlessness of mutability by the paradoxical
laws of the Garden. But our feelings shift when Spenser
picks out a particular object as an example of this process. Far different to accept the universe than to watch
the lily fade; the first is grand because it allows for both
the beautiful and the hateful, while the second is devastating:

> *Great enimy to it, and to all the rest,*
> *That in the Gardin of Adonis springs,*
> *Is wicked Tyme, who, with his scyth addrest,*
> *Does mow the flowring herbes and goodly things,*
> *And all their glory to the ground downe flings,*
> *Where they do wither and are fowly mard:*
> *He flyes about, and with his flaggy winges*
> *Beates downe both leaves and buds without regard,*
> *Ne ever pitty may relent his malice hard.*
>
> (III,vi,39)

For six lines Time is a reaper grimly mowing down the pastoral scenery of herbs, leaves, buds, and goodly things. Then the image changes to Time as flying, not an enemy but merely obeying its own laws. Then the two are fused, "and with his flaggy winges Beates downe" so that the motion of flying is also an act of destruction; the wings beat impersonally, "without regard," yet also they are malicious and will not relent. Then, with one of his best repetitions, Spenser has Time as the reaper give way to a mourning for his victims:

> Yet pitty often did the gods relent,
> To see so faire thinges mard and spoiled quight:
> And their great mother Venus did lament
> The losse of her deare brood, her deare delight:
> Her hart was pierst with pitty at the sight,
> When walking through the gardin them she saw,
> Yet no'te she find redresse for such despight:
> For all that lives is subject to that law:
> All things decay in time, and to their end doe draw.
>
> (III,vi,40)

Venus, mother of all the fair things that Time destroys, loves, and yet even with this power she is unable to do more than lament "When walking through the gardin them she saw." As Venus becomes Dame Nature she nonetheless has her effect, for the very fact of pity modulates our sense of Time. For now we are dealing with a law and not malice: "All things decay in time, and to their end doe draw." Given this metaphorical intercession of Venus, Time is capable only of bringing created things to their due close. Even though Time beats down, the form is all that fades and "The sub-staunce is not chaungd nor altered." So Time, like chaos and the uncouth forms earlier, only seems horrible, and in fact it is part of a law larger than it:

> *But were it not, that Time their troubler is,*
> *All that in this delightfull gardin growes*
> *Should happy bee, and have immortall blis:*
> *For here all plenty and all pleasure flowes,*
> *And sweete Love gentle fitts emongst them throwes,*
> *Without fell.rancor or fond gealosy:*
> *Franckly each paramor his leman knowes,*
> *Each bird his mate, ne any does envy*
> *Their goodly meriment and gay felicity.*
>
> (III,vi,41)

In this kind of writing, with the subject and tone modulating almost every stanza, the last thing we can expect is "consistency." After paying his final homage to Time, Spenser ignores it. Cupid's hurling of his darts is transformed: "Love gentle fitts emongst them throwes," so that instead of the wandering we have seen up to this moment, we have: "Franckly each paramor his leman knowes." The shift is possible because we have come to see the Garden as the place where Nature and Love are one. Time the destroyer has been transformed into a lawful thing, cruel but controlled, and the moment we see this we see what has been hitherto unknown in Book III—openness, frankness, twoness—this is what growth is:

> *There is continuall spring, and harvest there*
> *Continuall, both meeting at one tyme:*
> *For both the boughes doe laughing blossoms beare,*
> *And with fresh colours decke the wanton pryme . . .*
>
> (III,vi,42)

Thus Time is transformed by pity and love into seasons: spring and fall are always there as they are always implicitly everywhere, so the tree has laughing blossoms and autumn colors simultaneously. Natural process becomes love as it orders time, and now even decay has its place. Having achieved this, Spenser moves into a hierarchy of lovers and, in two of his greatest stanzas, he links love and process in a sexual image which time and mortality can never destroy:

> There wont fayre Venus often to enjoy
> Her deare Adonis joyous company,
> And reape sweet pleasure of the wanton boy:
> There yet, some say, in secret he does ly,
> Lapped in flowres and pretious spycery,
> By her hid from the world, and from the skill
> Of Stygian gods, which doe her love envy;
> But she her selfe, when ever that she will,
> Possesseth him, and of his sweetnesse takes her fill.
>
> (III,vi,46)

This is Venus as she is always thought of ideally, not Dame Nature or the anxious mother of Cupid, but triumphant lover, hidden, but only from the envious; the reference to Stygian gods offers brief acknowledgment of a fallen world, then Spenser moves on to the last line, miraculously both anatomically explicit and completely joyous. The joy of her love resides in her lover, in whose garden she moves:

> And sooth, it seemes, they say: for he may not
> For ever dye, and ever buried bee
> In balefull night, where all thinges are forgot;
> All be he subject to mortalitie,
> Yet is eterne in mutabilitie,
> And by succession made perpetuall,
> Transformed oft, and chaunged diverslie:

> *For him the father of all formes they call;*
> *Therfore needs mote he live, that living gives to all.*
>
> (III,vi,47)

This is rightly considered one of the poem's great moments—the Garden becomes not only human but mortal. As succession is made perpetual, history is transformed from chronicle to human process; "eterne" answers "mutabilitie" and the last line gives the reason: Adonis must live because he gives life. Venus is again Dame Nature, and as she takes her fill of his sweetness father joins mother, mortal becomes immortal, natural process is made love.

As the father of forms Adonis becomes a kind of immortal, and the boar that subjects him is also subjected, "Hewen underneath that mount, that none him losen may." With beautiful clarity, Spenser shows that thus to "emprison" the boar, the symbol of the lover's mortality, is to deny Cupid his darts, the symbols of the lover's pain. Seldom has Spenser or anyone moved so confidently among the implications of the ancient stories:

> *and laying his sad dartes*
> *Asyde, with faire Adonis playes his wanton partes.*
>
> (III,vi,49)

The next stanza easily picks up the image:

> *And his trew love, faire Psyche, with him playes,*
> *Fayre Psyche to him lately reconcyld . . .*
>
> (III,vi,50)

After love becomes generation, love is married to the soul, but produces nothing more ethereal than Pleasure. This is not a hierarchy if we mean by that a progression from lesser to greater; it is a hierarchy because Venus and Adonis are a precondition of Cupid and Psyche,

and they, in turn, are a precondition of their child,
Pleasure, and their adopted daughter Amoret. Amoret is
not "the peak" of anything; she is only where we inevitably come out; she is the most human-like of the
figures in the Garden, not a universal principle but an
educable girl:

> In which when she to perfect ripenes grew,
> Of grace and beautie noble paragone,
> She brought her forth into the worldes vew,
> To be th' ensample of true love alone,
> And lodestarre of all chaste affection
> To all fayre ladies, that doe live on grownd.
>
> (III,vi,52)

The process is different from the earlier "bringing forth"
from the Garden. Amoret emerges as a symbol, an embodiment of chaste affection rather than a simple participant in the eternal movement of birth, growth, and decay.
Whatever she represents, she is, like her sister Belphoebe,
a lady. It would not do to stress the distinction between
"mortal" and "immortal" when speaking of the daughters
of Chrysogonee and the sun, but it can be said that
for Amoret we have a story, a kind of biography, which
is something we could not possibly have for Venus or
Cupid. Venus in the Garden is Dame Nature, love as
natural process, and so is only incidentally human.
Amoret, by comparison, is strictly human, "trained up in
trew feminitee," sent to Faerie court, destined to become
the sworn lover of Scudamour. She is, if we like, the
civilized embodiment of Venus, the distilled human
result of the cosmic processes of the Garden.

Then, at the end of the canto Spenser announces he
is going to return to Florimell, whom he had left fleeing
from Arthur. After the huge serene vision of the Garden,

which has brought us to a fuller understanding than before of the nature that is love, we return and see that, in one sense, nothing has changed in Faerie Land. *We* see more, *we* know differently, yet we do not really see. It is the assurance of Spenser's sequence that visions of universality do not change the lot of human life; Florimell is still running and is still subject to all the dangers and fears as before. So we know the world is larger than we had known, but also that mutability is always with us, shifting, altering, and preventing us from maintaining the visions we would carry with us if we could. The Garden has not done away with evil or even concerned itself with evil. It offers no way of dealing easily with the hardness and terrors of life for it is not a "place" to which we can escape. As we move into Canto vii and beyond, the Garden lingers in the mind as all the great things in the poem do, but that is all. Adventures, grand and otherwise, are unavoidable.

Perhaps the most important fact about the next two cantos is that stanzas begin with lines like: "Like as an hynd forth singled from the heard," or "All that same evening she in flying spent," or "And forst t'alight, on foot mote algates fare." These can be compared with an analogous moment in a work more completely engrossed in a fictional world, Chaucer's *Troilus*. Here is the opening of the fourth book, which follows the joyous union in Book III and precedes Criseyde's departure and betrayal:

> But al to litel, weylawey the whyle,
> Lasteth swich joie, ythonked be Fortune,
> That seemeth trewest whan she wol bygyle

Comic irony is all that is available to Chaucer: Fortune beguiles, joy lasts such a short time. In *The Faerie*

Queene Florimell's running "comes after" the Garden of Adonis, but not in the same way that Criseyde's betrayal "comes after" the night of love with Troilus. For in the sense that the Garden of Adonis is "there," it is always there; its truths are not altered by Florimell's plight. But Spenser needs no comic irony because his vision demands no resignation; that Florimell must fly and the palfrey must tire shows only that these events too are part of the vision as surely as is the Garden. We have watched the mist that surrounds and partially blinds human beings gradually lift through Cantos v and vi, but it is only our watching that has changed; the characters and the universe are as they have always been. Because the Garden is a drawing together of things that have been operative in more scattered ways earlier, many writers have tried to see it as a dividing line and to detect a change between the first six and the last six cantos of Book III. Unquestionably there are differences, and we must stress them, but we can do this only after having insisted on the evenness of Spenser's tone that is neither more delighted nor more dismayed at Florimell than at Amoret in the Garden; all is true, one truth does not take precedence over another. We read on, we change, but Faerie Land does not.

But Cantos vii and viii do mark a shift in emphasis. The lonely condition of the lover is the major strand in the first six cantos, while here the confrontations of characters are more open, complete, and destructive. The witch's son falls in love with Florimell just as did the earlier lovers:

> *But tears, nor charms, nor herbs, nor counsell might*
> *Asswage the fury which his entrails teares:*
> *So strong is passion that no reason heares.*
>
> (III,vii,21)

But the son is not, as Marinell was, left by his mother
to suffer his fate and his love. It may seem that Spenser
is much harder on the witch's son—"wicked sonne,"
"lewd lover," a creature of "base thought" and "feeble
eyne"—than on the others who were also only victims.
But Spenser is not in the business of judging characters
as such, of saying "Britomart is my heroine so what
she does is all right" or "the witch's son is an uncouth
lout and so I will be harsh to him." He is, rather, only
taking the same or similar passion and putting it in a
somewhat harsher light. He does this by emphasizing
Florimell's helplessness, but even more by moving from
son to mother. The witch, though moved by Florimell at
first, only wants to destroy her after she escapes—and
Florimell is in a position where she can only submit or
fly—so she "helps" her son by releasing the beast "That
feeds on wemens flesh, as others feede on gras." The
malice of the witch and the beast is open and avowed,
not accidental like Britomart's attack on Marinell. Florimell flees to the shore, escapes in the fisherman's boat,
but her palfrey is left to be slaughtered:

> The monster, ready on the pray to sease,
> Was of his forward hope deceived quight,
> Ne durst assay to wade the perlous seas,
> But, greedily long gaping at the sight,
> At last in vaine was forst to turne his flight,
> And tell the idle tidings to his dame:
> Yet, to avenge his divelishe despight,
> He sett upon her palfrey tired lame,
> And slew him cruelly, ere any reskew came.
>
> (III,vii,28)

The open, ruttish desperate pursuit and destruction of
beauty has taken the place of the painful, lost, wandering
hunting of Britomart and Arthur.

Then, just as Britomart and Arthur were followed by
the rescuing Belphoebe, so the witch and the beast are
followed by the virgin knight Palladine, who is chasing
the giantess Argante and her captive, the Squire of
Dames. Finally, in the Squire's story of the birth of
Argante and Ollyphant, we have a kind of parody of
the birth of Amoret and Belphoebe:

> 'For at that berth another babe she bore,
> To weet, the mightie Ollyphant, that wrought
> Great wreake to many errant knights of yore,
> And many hath to foule confusion brought.
> These twinnes, men say, (a thing far passing thought)
> Whiles in their mothers wombe enclosd they were,
> Ere they into the lightsom world were brought,
> In fleshly lust were mingled both yfere,
> And in that monstrous wise did to the world appere.'
>
> (III,vii,48)

The grand processes of the Garden are here perverted, the
twin birth of natural virginity and "trew feminitee"
becomes the mingling of Argante and Ollyphant which
leads to a wild nymphomania that appalls even the
libertine Squire. This is Malecasta without a redeeming
quality of sophistication:

> 'Who, not content so fowly to devoure
> Her native flesh, and staine her brothers bowre,
> Did wallow in all other fleshly myre,
> And suffred beastes her body to deflowre,
> So whot she burned in that lustfull fyre:
> Yet all that might not slake her sensuall desyre.'
>
> (III,vii,49)

Where Malecasta seeks open subjection or secret conquest, Argante is only in a state of nature, physical, out of control, monstrous in her insatiability. She may be in one sense less culpable than Malecasta—hers is not a willed perversion—but also she can evoke no pity or shame.

Then comes the Squire of Dames' story of his exploits. He looks much like the other squire, Timias: "a comely personage, And lovely face." But it is a face made to deceive. His tale of the three hundred ladies who submit to him and the three who do not is a version of Ariosto's tale of Jocondo, but here it primarily complements his story of Argante. Josephine Waters Bennett finds that these stories are awkwardly stitched into the fabric of the poem; they are among the first parts of the poem Spenser wrote and he merely found a place for them somewhere.[4] But surely the point is that the women the Squire of Dames meets are only more subtle than the monster, and surely this implicit cynicism is not the unpardonable sin Hawthorne's Ethan Brand found his cynicism to be, but only the first and most primitive response to the discovery of natural monstrousness; the tone is best set when Satyrane calls the Squire's exploits one of the labors of Hercules. The fact that Spenser wrote this story long before he wrote the cantos on either side of it does not alter the more important fact that he knew what to do with it; in a landscape of parody, the Squire's deeds are heroic exploits.

Finally, in the next canto, we have the epitome of parody, the snowy Florimell manufactured by the witch to assuage the pain of her lovesick son. Cymoent protected her son from his Florimell because she listened to Proteus, but the witch can go prophecy one better:

[4] *The Evolution of "The Faerie Queene"* (Chicago: University of Chicago Press, 1942), pp. 138–153.

> *A wicked spright, yfraught with fawning guyle*
> *And fayre resemblance, above all the rest*
> *Which with the Prince of Darkenes fell somewhyle*
> *From heavens blis and everlasting rest . . .*
>
> (III,viii,8)

God makes Eve for Adam, a fallen spright makes a
Florimell for the witch, and he needs no instructions
either. What nature cannot provide, man manufactures.
But the false Florimell is not "born" to be with a peasant.
She finds her knightly counterpart in Bragadocchio, and
she "made him thinke him selfe in heven, that was in
hell." Milton's sense of Pandemonium as a parody of
Heaven is no more secure than Spenser's.

All these parallels between the characters here and in
the earlier cantos are easily made but need not be insisted upon. Some are clear, like the two Florimells, but
others, like Cymoent and the witch, are fainter. But at
best they only restate what the cantos make clear by
themselves—that Spenser is filling his world with open
and confessed perversions as a dark image of the Garden
of Adonis. If the remarkable quality of the first six
cantos is the absence of enemies, the dominant qualities
here are the absence of heroism and the helplessness of
those not perverted, debauched, or cynical. That is why
these are Florimell's cantos: she is fearful and helpless,
subject to the whims and assaults of anyone she meets:

> *But Florimell her selfe was far away,*
> *Driven to great distresse by fortune straunge,*
> *And taught the carefull mariner to play,*
> *Sith late mischaunce had her compeld to chaunge*
> *The land for sea, at randon there to raunge . . .*
>
> (III,viii,20)

Strange fortune, mischance, and random wandering—all
these words could apply to Britomart in the early cantos
of Book III, but a strong response is always available to
her. The responses, of course, lead to comic folly and
barbarous assault, but that is because Britomart cannot
see or know what is happening. Florimell, however,
is assaulted and kidnapped openly, yet the unsubtlety
of her assailants helps not at all. She is captured by the
fisherman, then "rescued" by Proteus. This is seen first
as the "soveraine favor towards chastity" of High God,
but the way in which the rescue shows the voluntary
grace of the heavens is not immediately clear. Florimell
has moved from the simple passion of the witch's son and
the lust of the fisherman to the more designing intent
of Proteus, and so she is moving further from the knights
who might save her to a world from which there seems
no escape:

> *Like as a fearefull partridge, that is fledd*
> *From the sharpe hauke, which her attached neare,*
> *And fals to ground, to seeke for succor theare,*
> *Whereas the hungry spaniells she does spye,*
> *With greedy jawes her ready for to teare;*
> *In such distresse and sad perplexity*
> *Was Florimell, when Proteus she did see thereby.*
>
> (III,viii,33)

Proteus is another great example of Spenser's almost
sublime ability to understand the implications of myths
and their potential use for his poem. Proteus is the
"shepheard of the seas of yore," the Old Man of the Sea,
and his home here is a version of his home in Virgil's
Georgics:

> *His bowre is in the bottom of the maine,*
> *Under a mightie rocke, gainst which doe rave*
> *The roring billowes in their proud disdaine,*
> *That with the angry working of the wave*
> *Therein is eaten out an hollow cave . . .*
>
> (III,viii,37)

But as the rescuer and would-be seducer of Florimell,
Proteus is a version of the Pluto who captured Persephone
and took her to the underworld. The Proteus of Homer
and Virgil is no seducer, but he can transform his shape;
Spenser's insight is to see this transforming as the eternal
activity of the lover:

> *Then like a Faerie knight him selfe he drest;*
> *For every shape on him he could endew:*
> *Then like a king he was to her exprest,*
> *And offred kingdoms unto her in vew,*
> *To be his leman and his lady trew . . .*
>
> (III,viii,40)

This is an underworld Adonis, the father of forms; he
combines in a single figure the image of mutability and
the image of the seducer, just as love and growth were
combined in Adonis. But while in the Garden Adonis
and Venus join in the process of making the mutable
eternal, here the processes are all on one side, Proteus',
and Florimell is isolated, alone, static, an image of lost
virtuous beauty. Proteus transforms himself into wilder
and more frightening shapes:

> *Now like a gyaunt, now like to a feend,*
> *Then like a centaure, then like to a storme,*
> *Raging within the waves: thereby he weend*

> *Her will to win unto his wished eend.*
> *But when with feare, nor favour, nor with all*
> *He els could doe, he saw him selfe esteemd,*
> *Downe in a dongeon deepe he let her fall,*
> *And threatned there to make her his eternall thrall.*
>
> (III,viii,41)

Of course for Proteus, as for Adonis, there is no "eend"; it is his fate to be eternally changing. Captivity to the god of transformation is precisely the fit end for Florimell, who has in effect been such a captive all along, chased by figures not in themselves protean but having that effect as one takes another's place in the pursuit: forester, then Guyon and Arthur, then witch's son and devouring beast, then fisherman. Florimell, the victim of *this* eternal mutability, isolated from all solace of cosmic or historical process, shows us precisely what happens when one is thus isolated. The most she can do is to refuse, for to join here with the processes is to lose virtue, and so all Spenser can do is to praise her:

> *Most vertuous virgin! glory be thy meed,*
> *And crowne of heavenly prayse with saintes above,*
> *Where most sweet hymmes of this thy famous deed*
> *Are still emongst them song, that far my rymes exceed.*
>
> (III,viii,42)

The whole point is that Florimell is not Persephone, that the power and will to resist are the sources of the glory that is her meed; her response is pathetic, but she needs no other. We do not, as we do with Britomart earlier, "see" or "understand" Florimell here—it is her fate to be only an image of fidelity and truth. She is grand because constant, unprotean, but because she is this, she is lost, lonely, eternally in thrall. Anyone inclined to feel there is something nigh inhuman in Florimell's refusal to submit to Proteus has seen what Spenser sees, but has missed his point.

We next move to the cantos that for me are the best in the poem and which rank with the greatest extended stretches of poetry in English. This does not mean they are somehow detachable as a unit, for in fact there is nothing particularly unified about them within themselves, and there is much that forces us to see them as a continuation of what precedes. But here in the stories of Malbecco and Busirane Spenser's sense of his vision is so crystalline that he seems able to express, as though there were no genius in doing so, the most profound and delicate awareness of the healths and sicknesses of sexuality. Here, perhaps more than anywhere else in the poem, what is most surprising is Spenser's lack of surprise at his own grandeur. Any break, any sense of surprise or rage or sudden fascination would inevitably carry with it a snicker or a salacious leer; not even the authors of *Othello* and *Paradise Lost* were as able to control their effects as securely as Spenser has here, to avoid the implication that they are authors peering at their own material.

The situation, if it can be so called, as we come to the House of Malbecco, is as follows: after the Garden of Adonis, Faerie Land is filled with what cynics love to call "the world"—defenseless Florimell, willing but ineffective Satyrane, lustful Argante, maliciously inventive witch, fake and beautiful Florimell, boastful Bragadocchio, courtly Paridell, uncouth fisherman, hoary and determined sea god Proteus. At the beginning of the ninth canto Satyrane, Paridell, and the Squire of Dames stop before Malbecco's gates and the Squire tells the others why they are not allowed in:

'But all his mind is set on mucky pelfe,
To hoord up heapes of evill gotten masse,
For which he others wrongs and wreckes himselfe;
Yet is he lincked to a lovely lasse,
Whose beauty doth her bounty far surpasse,
The which to him both far unequall yeares
And also far unlike conditions has;
For she does joy to play emongst her peares,
And to be free from hard restraynt and gealous feares.'

(III,ix,4)

This is the situation Chaucer loved to describe, but
Spenser makes clear what is never quite as clear in
"The Merchant's Tale"—that jealousy is not so much
the claim made by one who has not on one who has, as it
is a miserly sense of private property. Malbecco treats
his wife as "mucky pelfe" and "evill gotten masse," and
the Squire knows full well she is not this but a "lovely
lasse" who loves to "play emongst her peares." The
Squire, of course, has no sense of private property at all:

'But he is old, and withered like hay,
Unfit faire ladies service to supply,
The privie guilt whereof makes him alway
Suspect her truth, and keepe continuall spy
Upon her with his other blincked eye;
Ne suffreth he resort of living wight
Approch to her, ne keepe her company,
But in close bowre her mewes from all mens sight,
Depriv'd of kindly joy and naturall delight.'

(III,ix,5)

The Squire sees no difference between *free* and *libertine*
and so his idea of "service" is simple and sexual, what
he calls "naturall." Malbecco is, thus, another version of
Proteus. In the cave the seducer is captor, whose "service"

is rebuffed, while here the captor only spies and blinks and keeps out those who would "serve." In the Squire's world Florimell is not imaginable.

Satyrane replies, and while he does not really have a higher view of women, he does view marriage differently:

> 'Extremely mad the man I surely deeme,
> That weenes with watch and hard restraynt to stay
> A womans will, which is disposd to go astray.'
>
> (III,ix,6)

What to the Squire is "naturall," "kindly joy," is to Satyrane a desire to "go astray." But it is left for Paridell to give the deepest interpretation:

> 'Then is he not more mad,' sayd Paridell,
> 'That hath himselfe unto such service sold,
> In dolefull thraldome all his dayes to dwell?
> For sure a foole I doe him firmely hold,
> That loves his fetters, though they were of gold.'
>
> (III,ix,8)

"That loves his fetters, though they were of gold"—a brilliant formulation in its insistence that Malbecco does not "serve" his wife because he serves another. It is good that the line is spoken by one whose response to the situation is to try to ransack the hall himself.

This conversation, like that between Venus and Diana in Canto vi, brings us out of the forests and sea caves and back into a realm where human discourse is possible, and in its neat redefinitions of Malbecco's situation it shows that the kinds of distinctions which Spenser has been making throughout are not unavailable to the characters. In its movement, too, we slowly see the jocular ease of the Squire and the solemn irrelevance of Satyrane pushed into the background, while the more civilized and sensitive Paridell moves forward. But immediately Spenser puts Paridell in the position of a Malbecco; a stranger knight rides up, is refused entrance, seeks to join the others in the shelter, and Paridell blocks the way. The knight knocks him down, Satyrane pacifies them both, and finally Malbecco lets them in and the stranger is revealed:

> *And eke that straunger knight emongst the rest*
> *Was for like need enforst to disaray:*
> *Tho, whenas vailed was her lofty crest,*
> *Her golden locks, that were in tramells gay*
> *Upbounden, did them selves adowne display,*
> *And raught unto her heeles; like sunny beames,*
> *That in a cloud their light did long time stay,*
> *Their vapour vaded, shewe their golden gleames,*
> *And through the persant aire shoote forth their*
>   *azure streames.*

(III,ix,20)

It does not matter that Spenser does not call the stranger Britomart for another eight stanzas. Nor does it really matter that this is her first appearance since the rain clouds enveloped her in Canto iv. Right in this canto there has been rain: "a bitter stormy blast, With showre and hayle so horrible and dred"; indeed, Paridell when he fights Britomart has been "like as a boystrous winde, . . . and skyes doth overcast." So now Britomart's enforced disarray brings with it the sudden appearance of the sun, a kind of woman Paridell, Satyrane, and the Squire know nothing about. First it is her natural grandeur that is stressed—her locks "them selves adowne display." In the next stanza it is her girlishness, "her well plighted frock, which she did won To tucke about her

short, when she did ryde," her "carelesse modestee" that
is the source of the marvel. Finally, it is her power as
knightly champion that makes the others look as "In
contemplation of divinitee":

> Like as Minerva, being late returnd
> From slaughter of the giaunts conquered;
> Where proud Encelade, whose wide nosethrils
>   burnd
> With breathed flames, like to a furnace redd,
> Transfixed with her speare, downe tombled dedd
> From top of Hemus, by him heaped hye;
> Hath loosd her helmet from her lofty hedd,
> And her Gorgonian shield gins to untye
> From her lefte arme, to rest in glorious victorye.
>
> (III,ix,22)

Britomart as natural sunlight, Britomart as a modest girl,
Britomart as the slaughterer of giants—neatly Spenser
boxes in the assumptions about women so casually held
by the others. Neither the courtly love of Paridell nor
the jealous love of Malbecco that follows will ever begin
to comprehend Britomart, and the more we see this the
more we will also be able to see that Paridell and Malbecco are, at bottom, one.

First we have Paridell, easily turning from his vision
of Britomart's divinity to his resumption of his usual occupation:

> And ever and anone, when none was ware,
> With speaking lookes, that close embassage bore,
> He rov'd at her, and told his secret care:
> For all that art he learned had of yore.
>
> (III,ix,28)

This is like Malecasta, but with an important difference.

Malecasta is helpless when beset by her passion, while Paridell's roving and "secret care" are only part of a carefully controlled art. Paridell is something new to Book III. Instead of the helplessness of Malecasta, Britomart, and Timias when struck with the dart of love, instead of the workmanlike cynicism of the Squire of Dames, instead of the natural beauty and grace of Belphoebe and Amoret, we have a civilized, controlled, and courtly acceptance of the pain:

> Ne was she ignoraunt of that leud lore,
> But in his eye his meaning wisely redd,
> And with the like him aunswerd evermore:
> Shee sent at him one fyrie dart, whose hedd
> Empoisned was with privy lust and gealous dredd.
>
> He from that deadly throw made no defence,
> But to the wound his weake heart opened wyde:
> The wicked engine through false influence
> Past through his eies, and secretly did glyde
> Into his heart, which it did sorely gryde.
>
> (III,ix,28–29)

This is civilization's reply to the unavoidable pain of love. This eager acceptance of what must seem the human condition is what we call courtly love, and in Paridell's response to Hellenore's assumption of Cupid's role we can see the result. He masters passion by willing it into existence so that it can be anticipated and controlled, even the lust, the dread, and the pain:

> But nothing new to him was that same paine,
> Ne paine at all; for he so ofte had tryde
> The powre thereof, and lov'd so oft in vaine,
> That thing of course he counted, love to entertaine.
>
> (III,ix,29)

Paridell makes us realize that since Canto i we have been outside human society, so to speak, on the plains and stronds, in the forests and gardens. If the universal processes are more easily seen there, nonetheless the individuals there are desperate and alone. For Paridell the wound is part of a scheme, his and all courtiers' answer to the Garden of Adonis:

> Thenceforth to her he sought to intimate
> His inward griefe, by meanes to him well knowne:
> Now Bacchus fruit out of the silver plate
> He on the table dasht, as overthrowne,
> Or of the fruitfull liquor overflowne,
> And by the dauncing bubbles did divine,
> Or therein write to lett his love be showne;
> Which well she redd out of the learned line:
> A sacrament prophane in mistery of wine.
>
> (III,ix,30)

The looks, the eating, the drinking and spilling, the writing of the "learned line" in the "dauncing bubbles"; the sacrament is profane, and terribly so, but the wine is as mysterious here as in the Eucharist. When such a figure is judged, it must not be done simply, on the grounds that he "does not really love Hellenore." Of course he doesn't, but he also touches on the brink of all we love.

Then follows Paridell's "gratious speach" which traces his ancestry. He describes the Paris who stole Helen from Menelaus (as Paridell is about to steal his Helen from Malbecco) as a knightly "Sir Paris" who "through great prowesse and bold hardinesse" "fetcht the fayrest dame" and was rewarded by Venus. The idea that Paris "fetcht" Helen is perfect here, for it shows that to Paridell, as much as to Malbecco, women are things, prizes, conquests, to be had and held rather than loved. Inextricably involved with the idea of knightly glory there is the idea of the infinite corruptibility of women; that is the profanity of Paridell's sacrament, and that is the reason that Spenser's central images of chastity are women too.

Britomart's answer to Paridell is not rebuke but another story of a different Troy. Her Venus does not reward the fetching of other men's wives, but is fruitful like the Venus of the Garden; she is the mother of Aeneas, who left Troy in flames to found a second such city:

> 'There, there,' said Britomart, 'a fresh appeard
> The glory of the later world to spring,
> And Troy againe out of her dust was reard,
> To sitt in second seat of soveraine king
> Of all the world under her governing.
> But a third kingdom yet is to arise
> Out of the Trojans scattered ofspring,
> That, in all glory and great enterprise,
> Both first and second Troy shall dare to equalise.'
>
> (III,ix,44)

This is like Merlin's prophecy, not a palliative to the present but a patriotic vision of possible human glory aware of danger and disaster; Troy is "ensample of mans wretched state, That floures so fresh at morne, and fades at evening late." The subject here is not chastity, though a great deal of Spenser's sense of chastity is expressed in this contrast between Britomart and Paridell. Britomart is solemn, Paridell is off-hand, she is patriotic and provincial, he his "native soile have lefte" to become a man of the world. After she offers her vision, Paridell replies in his best courtly drawl. He assures her it was only clumsy oversight that made him forget her history, he has heard of Troynovant and Lincoln and Cleopolis and all the best cities. Aeneas had described his destiny to

Dido after dinner, and so does Britomart here, but what for them was solemn is for him merely the conversation of a raconteur. There is nothing his urbanity cannot accommodate. His acceptance of Britomart is like his welcome of the dart of love—easy, gracious, knowing, and (so the next canto will assure us if we did not know already), indifferent. Spenser is quite clear that such "service" to all is service to nothing, yet he never openly condemns Paridell here, either by praising Britomart or by attacking courtliness. The tone of the passage is close to high comedy, and it is wonderful that he is able to keep Britomart solemn without making her seem a boor. Paridell belongs in *Orlando Furioso* as Britomart never could, but here they fit together in a fine tableau. The grimmer consequences of Paridell's way of the world are for later, as are Britomart's heroic responses to them.

For now Britomart and Satyrane leave Malbecco's and Paridell is free to rape his host's willing wife. As Canto ix leans towards high comedy, as Cantos xi–xii towards a religious enactment of romance, so Canto x moves into the grotesque. First comes the courtly wooing:

> He sigh'd, he sobd, he swownd, he perdy dyde,
> And cast himselfe on ground her fast besyde:
> Tho, when againe he him bethought to live,
> He wept, and wayld, and false laments belyde,
> Saying, but if she mercie would him give,
> That he mote algates dye, yet did his death forgive.
>
> (III,x,7)

This is Chaucer's Troilus, Shakespeare's Romeo of Act I, Dryden's Antony, but Spenser is clear that its solemnity is false and its lovesickness only a civilized game:

> *And otherwhyles with amorous delights*
> *And pleasing toyes he would her entertaine,*
> *Now singing sweetly, to surprize her sprights,*
> *Now making layes of love and lovers paine,*
> *Bransles, ballads, virelayes, and verses vaine . . .*
>
> (III,x,8)

The voraciousness of the pursuers of Florimell has been modulated into a deceitful art: "Thus finely did he his false nets dispred." But, and here is perhaps Spenser's clearest insight coming through again, take away the art and the passion is modulated into the comedy of Malbecco:

> *Into huge waves of griefe and gealosye*
> *Full deepe emplonged was, and drowned nye*
> *Twixt inward doole and felonous despight:*
> *He rav'd, he wept, he stampt, he lowd did cry,*
> *And all the passions that in man may light*
> *Did him attonce oppresse, and vex his caytive spright.*
>
> (III,x,17)

Throughout Canto ix and thus far in Canto x Spenser has avoided weaving abstract nouns and sprights with the usual denizens of his Faerie Land, and has adapted the Chaucerian scene to his own more somber comedy. But here the sprights return and we see that they have been kept out because that is Paridell's art, and that as Paridell sighs, sobs, swoons, and almost dies, he is only playing at Malbecco's raving, weeping, stamping, and loud crying. Both seek to control life by possessing it, both treat Hellenore as an object, which is exactly how she treats herself. But as we move out of this scenic rendering and back into something like Spenser's more usual

manner, the transformations are more marked and shocking than they would have been otherwise. First we have
the encounter of Malbecco with Bragadocchio and Trompart where the braggart unknowingly offers an accurate
judgment of Malbecco—"Thou clod of vilest clay"—and
Malbecco is reduced by such rhetoric to offering what he
most prizes as a reward for regaining what he cannot
have to one who cannot possibly get it for him. Then
Spenser pauses to offer a strikingly terse judgment of
Paridell, who rides by alone:

> For having filcht her bells, her up he cast
> To the wide world, and let her fly alone;
> He nould be clogd. So had he served many one.
>
> (III,x,35)

Back he moves to Malbecco and the satyrs, the man now
become a horned goat:

> Which when Malbecco saw, out of his bush
> Upon his hands and feete he crept full light,
> And like a gote emongst the gotes did rush,
> That through the helpe of his faire hornes on hight,
> And misty dampe of misconceyving night,
> And eke through likenesse of his gotish beard,
> He did the better counterfeite aright . . .
>
> (III,x,47)

Of the countless uses of the cuckold's horns in medieval
and Renaissance literature, this is perhaps the one that
takes the metaphor most literally. Malbecco, we notice,
is in a position where he seeks to become a goat, to hide
the fact he is a man; this is the way he can love:

> At night, when all they went to sleepe, he vewd
> Whereas his lovely wife emongst them lay,

Embraced of a Satyre rough and rude,
Who all the night did minde his joyous play:
Nine times he heard him come aloft ere day,
That all his hart with gealosy did swell;
But yet that nights ensample did bewray,
That not for nought his wife them loved so well,
When one so oft a night did ring his matins bell.

                                        (III,x,48)

The comedy here accommodates the sardonic praise of
Hellenore for loving at last so lusty a mate, and also
makes clear that Malbecco's voyeurism is a kind of love—
"That all his hart with gealosy did swell." Malbecco,
twitching and blinking, seeks out his wife and seeks to
persuade her that *her* life is loathsome and that he will
forgive *her* if she will return with him. She refuses, he
rejoins the goats who trample him. He flees to rejoin his
treasure, but that too is gone, and so he runs and runs:

High over hilles and over dales he fledd,
As if the wind him on his winges had borne,
Ne banck nor bush could stay him, when he spedd
His nimble feet, as treading still on thorne:
Griefe, and despight, and gealosy, and scorne
Did all the way him follow hard behynd,
And he himselfe himselfe loath'd so forlorne,
So shamefully forlorne of womankynd;
That, as a snake, still lurked in his wounded mynd.

                                        (III,x,55)

The comedy has disappeared and the sprights have returned in the form of furies chasing Malbecco. Yet even
now, deformed and transformed, he cannot stop hating
himself or remembering that he was abandoned. He is
joining the abstractions now, becoming one himself; as

he jumps off a cliff to destroy himself, his pain and "selfe-murdring thought" keep the suicide unconsummated:

> He was so wasted and forpined quight,
> That all his substance was consum'd to nought,
> And nothing left, but like an aery spright . . .
> (III,x,57)

Having lost his substance Malbecco ceases to be a person, and Spenser ushers him into the realm of the ghastly eternal:

> Into the same he creepes, and thenceforth there
> Resolv'd to build his balefull mansion,
> In drery darkenes, and continuall feare
> Of that rocks fall, which ever and anon
> Threates with huge ruine him to fall upon,
> That he dare never sleepe, but that one eye
> Still ope he keepes for that occasion . . .
> (III,x,58)

As the tense moves into the present Malbecco is no longer a man with a story. This is what it is like to be a spright—a blinking eye that always is suspicious, dangerous, filled with enmity. From here it is only a short step and he is a full allegorical figure:

> Yet can he never dye, but dying lives,
> And doth himselfe with sorrow new sustaine,
> That death and life attonce unto him gives,
> And painefull pleasure turnes to pleasing paine.
> There dwels he ever, miserable swaine,
> Hatefull both to him selfe and every wight;
> Where he, through privy griefe and horrour vaine,
> Is woxen so deform'd, that he has quight
> Forgot he was a man, and Gelosy is hight.
> (III,x,60)

First we have the machinery of eternal horror, a horrible parody of the Garden of Adonis: sorrow keeps creating itself in a birth that is, by its very loathing and self-destructiveness, a dying as well. Then comes the grim reminder that this is, after all, what Malbecco seeks; to gain pleasure through pain is the psychic counterpart of the "natural" process of birth and death. Then "There dwels he ever, miserable swaine," and Spenser swoops to include in Malbecco the courtly lover in a lovely gesture of sympathy and acknowledged humanity, and this is done before the man disappears—"Forgot he was a man" —and the allegorical figure emerges—"and Gelosy is hight." This is a supreme instance of the great power of the undramatic writer to shift, turn, and redefine freely, thereby making a myth. For in the descent of Malbecco is also the ascent to abstraction, and so what is personally grotesque and grim in Malbecco is transformed into what is best called the restless and self-destructive desire for possession in all of us.

The close of the canto is so spectacular that it almost obscures the fact that its story, when placed in our usual ways of thinking about sexual love and chastity, is almost a subtype. Jealousy and cuckoldry are comic, after all, because their wounds are almost entirely self-inflicted and self-absorbed; even the bestial anguish of the witch's son and the passion of Argante carry with them a sense of a feeling for a larger world than oneself. It is only a later era that could believe that in love all wounds are self-inflicted and self-absorbing; for Spenser the greater evils and triumphs lie in a world more populous. But having reached a plane of abstraction at the end of Canto x, he can move easily onto the hard high ground of romance.

It would be wrong to speak of Britomart's rescue of Amoret as the climax of Book III because that would

imply narrative connections between these cantos and the
ones preceding which do not exist, or else thematic connections which do exist, but indirectly and by implication.
What can be said is that the last two cantos recomplete
the action of the whole book by clarifying something we
have known indirectly all along about Britomart, chastity,
and sexuality. The form of Book III or of any book in
the poem is too loose and too expansive for us ever to
reach—or need to want to reach—a moment where we
can see "what chastity is." But just as the Garden of
Adonis focused for us Spenser's reply to the aloneness of
the lover by means of a myth of growth, so the House of
Busirane focuses Spenser's reply to the evil and perversion
that besets beauty and chastity by means of Britomart's
romantic heroism. We could go on here and construct
diagrams and graphs of all the themes and show the way
they are orchestrated, and indeed it is often fun to do so
in order to gain a sense of the intricacy of Spenser's organization. But it is not such intricacy, really, that is
surprising or important—almost anyone who writes on a
series of related subjects can achieve as much. What is far
more important is the triumphant clarity of the linear
motion of the stanzas and cantos so that at almost any
one moment, we *can* stop and relate the stanza before
us to many that have preceded, yet what we *do* do, when
Spenser is as good as he is here, is to read the next stanza,
and the next, to see the Faerie world gather, complete,
and recomplete itself. If Malbecco can be transformed by
his anguished passion into an allegorical figure of jealousy,
the next "step" is to show such metamorphoses on a larger
scale, much as the Garden of Adonis follows Belphoebe's
transformation into a rose at the very end of Canto v.
In Canto vi, however, the modulation "upward" from
particular to abstract is also a modulation "upward" from

human loneliness and powerlessness to an image of mutability as growth. Here the transformation "upward" towards the abstract and the godlike is also a transformation "downward" from the godlike to the bestial, and from the glittering and grand to the cruel and the captive. This necessitates, as it were, an "answer" to Cupid and Busirane that is not part of the transforming process itself, and this answer is the heroic opposition of Britomart. We have seen Spenser offering parodies of the Garden of Adonis and the lovesick chaste Britomart. These dark images are here generalized in the tapestries and the masque; the lust of the witch's son, the twin giants, and the fisherman is now the lust of Jove and Apollo, and the courtly dalliance of the Squire of Dames and Paridell is the pageant that begins with Ease and ends with Shame. But Britomart stands outside the process, and in her great speech to the despairing Scudamour outside Busirane's castle she implicitly offers Spenser's reply to the process:

> *'Ah! gentle knight, whose deepe conceived griefe*
> *Well seemes t' exceede the powre of patience,*
> *Yet if that hevenly grace some good reliefe*
> *You send, submit you to High Providence,*
> *And ever in your noble hart prepense,*
> *That all the sorrow in the world is lesse*
> *Then vertues might and values confidence.*
> *For who nill bide the burden of distresse*
> *Must not here thinke to live: for life is*
>   *wretchednesse.'*

(III,xi,14)

"Yet if that hevenly grace"—it may not, but it may, send relief. Regardless, there is no grief greater than virtue, but one must know this completely, for only then can one bide the burden of the wretchedness of life. Scuda-

mour has cause for grief, and because relief is only a
possibility, one cannot control the burden, like a Paridell,
but can only bide it.

In one sense, as always, we have known the truth of
this from the beginning. Book III is strewn with figures
who felt the burden but gave in or sought to master it.
In another sense, as always, this is new, and not simply
because it articulates something never stated earlier. For
this reply to the wretchedness of life is human and
heroic. It does not, as Merlin did, turn to historical vision,
and it does not, as did the Garden of Adonis, show how
human life fits into the cosmos. The clarion call is clear—
no sorrow is great enough for "vertues might and values
confidence." What creates that power and confidence is,
of course, larger than human—history, cosmos, High
Providence. But its animating spirit is the human voice—
stern, wise, heroic.

This is not a new Britomart, but she is less of a shy
girl than before and more of the knightly hero Spenser
has claimed all along but has so seldom shown. It might
be possible to stitch together her several appearances and
show a kind of biographical education, but even if that
were desirable, the stitching would all unravel when we
come to her steps into the fire:

> Her ample shield she threw before her face,
> And her swords point directing forward right,
> Assayld the flame, the which eftesoones gave place,
> And did it selfe divide with equall space,
> That through she passed, as a thonder bolt
> Perceth the yielding ayre . . .
>
> (III,xi,25)

Her power is that of the magically endowed romantic
hero, a Tristram or a Sir Gawain, and added to this is the

sense, though the fact is never stated, that Britomart's sword and shield are illustrative of her chastity. If we seek to know how this magic is possible, our only answer is that she can divide the flames because she has bided the burden of distress—she knows not only what life is but how and how much to do about it.

Then come the tapestries, first described in a spectacular stanza that gave Pope his definition of the alexandrine:

> For round about, the walls yclothed were
> With goodly arras of great majesty,
> Woven with gold and silke so close and nere,
> That the rich metall lurked privily,
> As faining to be hidd from envious eye;
> Yet here, and there, and every where unwares
> It shewd it selfe, and shone unwillingly;
> Like a discolourd snake, whose hidden snares
> Through the greene gras his long bright burnisht
> back declares.

(III,xi,28)

Here is Spenser's whole sense of the awful mystery to be described; the tapestry becomes a snake yet remains a tapestry. Moving from "lurked" and "faining to be hidd," through "shewd it selfe" to the unwilling shining, the stanza enacts its sense of the powerful poison of the tapestries; the snake insinuates its way out of the arras and drags its slow length along, suggesting fatal, capricious powers as the green turns to gold.

The mythic counterpart of this beast is the Cupid whose victorious "cruell battailes" are "repeated" in the pictures in the tapestries. The arrangement is such that we realize only gradually just how cruel and triumphant Cupid is. First come the splendid metamorphoses of Jove, and the god transformed is still godlike: "And leaving heavens kingdome, here did rove In straunge disguize, to slake his scalding smart":

> *Then was he turnd into a snowy swan,*
> *To win faire Leda to his lovely trade:*
> *O wondrous skill and sweet wit of the man,*
> *That her in daffadillies sleeping made,*
> *From scorching heat her daintie limbes to shade:*
> *Whiles the proud bird, ruffing his fethers wyde*
> *And brushing his faire brest, did her invade!*
> *Shee slept, yet twixt her eielids closely spyde*
> *How towards her he rusht, and smiled at his pryde.*
>
> (III,xi,32)

This is not Venus and Adonis in the Garden, but neither is it Paridell and Hellenore. Jove may seem prouder of himself than he is interested in Leda, but Spenser's awe is shared by Leda, whose spying carries with it as much a sense of wonder as it does of wantonness.

Apollo comes next and the consequences of loving mortals become grimmer:

> *So lovedst thou the lusty Hyacinct,*
> *So lovedst thou the faire Coronis deare:*
> *Yet both are of thy haplesse hand extinct,*
> *Yet both in flowres doe live, and love thee beare,*
> *The one a paunce, the other a sweet breare:*
> *For griefe whereof, ye mote have lively seene*
> *The god himselfe rending his golden heare,*
> *And breaking quite his garlond ever greene,*
> *With other signes of sorrow and impatient teene.*
>
> (III,xi,37)

Though the mortals are of Apollo's hapless hand extinct, they at least live as flowers and still love, but Apollo is left, cursed almost with his immortality, "breaking quite his garlond ever greene." Still more pathetic is Neptune, who is the lord of the seas for a stanza and a half, then in four lines becomes a clownish lover:

> *The god himselfe did pensive seeme and sad,*
> *And hong adowne his head, as he did dreame:*
> *For privy love his brest empierced had,*
> *Ne ought but deare Bisaltis ay could make him glad.*
>
> (III,xi,41)

Jove and Apollo move as gods even in bestiality and jealous grief, but Neptune forsakes all he is and becomes smitten, powerless, all done for a mere "deare Bisaltis."

Finally comes the victor of the gods, blind Cupid led on by a blind dragon, "And all the people in that ample hous Did to that image bowe their humble knee, And oft committed fowle idolatree." The last phrase here may seem moralistic, but Spenser does not want so much to insist on a moral point as to contrast and finally combine it with Britomart's awed response, which follows:

> *That wondrous sight faire Britomart amazd,*
> *Ne seeing could her wonder satisfie,*
> *But ever more and more upon it gazd,*
> *The whiles the passing brightnes her fraile sences*
>   *dazd.*
>
> (III,xi,49)

Britomart is neither seduced nor priggish. Earlier she too was struck down by Cupid, but if she is to act heroically that must be ignored and no shock of recognition is possible. For her to feel that the worship portrayed in the tapestries is "fowle idolatree" would be to destroy their sense of mystery and wonder, yet to implicate her now would damn her quite unnecessarily. There is plenty of danger here without that:

And all about, the glistring walles were hong
With warlike spoiles and with victorious prayes
Of mightie conquerours and captaines strong,
Which were whilome captived in their dayes
To cruell Love, and wrought their owne decayes:
Their swerds and speres were broke, and hauberques
rent,
And their proud girlonds of tryumphant bayes
Troden in dust with fury insolent,
To shew the victors might and mercilesse intent.

(III,xi,52)

This second room is the end of it all, the trophy room of
the powerful, grand, mysterious god. Paridell plays loose
and frivolous games, but Cupid masters the universe, and
the "mercilesse intent" of his "fury insolent" is visible
here, beyond pain and false worship, a room without
people or human feeling.

The two mottoes, "Be bold" and "Be not too bold" most
simply state the dictatorial progress. "Be bold" we know
all about—it is the command to lovers. Lurking behind
the will to be strong and courageous is the snake-like
truth that the greater the boldness the greater the powerlessness and ultimate submission to Cupid. "Be not too
bold" is more difficult. It implies a standard of excess
which it does not state, and so the command is rationally
absurd, like the statement "Don't drive too fast." But the
very fact that the standard is unstated means that the
power to decide is in the hands of one who does not
need to draw fixed boundary lines, and whose power is so
pervasive it can decide at any moment to strike. Though
Britomart does not know what the intent is, Spenser
makes clear that at the moment her only possible response
is simply waiting in this nightmare atmosphere:

Thus she there wayted untill eventyde,
Yet living creature none she saw appeare:
And now sad shadowes gan the world to hyde
From mortall vew, and wrap in darkenes dreare;
Yet nould she d'off her weary armes, for feare
Of secret daunger, ne let sleepe oppresse
Her heavy eyes with natures burdein deare,
But drew her selfe aside in sickernesse,
And her welpointed wepons did about her dresse.

(III,xi,55)

The oppression of sleep and night, however dark they are, are "natures burdein deare," because the oppression here in the halls is far different.

Canto xii opens without a break from the preceding and, after the storm, the masque of Cupid begins. In part the movement of the masque reenacts that of the tapestries and goes from the seductive to the sadistic, and at a few points one can make rather close connections between the separate panels and the individual allegorical figures in the masque. But the reenacting is all on the level of human feelings, as in medieval allegories of love, and here Amoret can appear, Britomart can act, and the sense of awe can be dispelled. The problem that is usually posed with the question "What is Amoret doing in the House of Busirane?" can be answered by looking at the progress of the masque itself. We move from entertaining Ease, the prologue, to Desire with his handful of sparks, mistrusting Doubt and dreadful Daunger—what is this but the sequence of falling in love, and Amoret is here because, in a sense, so are we all. Not that everyone falls in love by moving through Ease to Feare to Cruelty and Despight, but it is a path we all recognize, and for Amoret to be there is only to say that the path is torturous,

Spenser's vision of the human lot. Amoret is a woman, and her weak passivity is at least implicitly a woman's trait when placed beside the cruel masculinity of her captor and torturer, but this is not a point stressed in the masque itself. Desire is represented as a man, Cruelty as a woman, Griefe a woman and Fury a man, and although the assignments of the sexes are made appropriate in their description, there is no suggestion that these traits are the exclusive property of one or the other sex.

We reach the climax of the masque in the description of Amoret's breast:

> Her brest all naked, as nett yvory,
> Without adorne of gold or silver bright,
> Wherewith the craftesman wonts it beautify,
> Of her dew honour was despoyled quight,
> And a wide wound therein (O ruefull sight!)
> Entrenched deep with knyfe accursed keene,
> Yet freshly bleeding forth her fainting spright,
> (The worke of cruell hand) was to be seene,
> That dyde in sanguine red her skin all snowy cleene.
>
> (III,xii,20)

Paul J. Alpers has written of the way this stanza involves the reader:

> When he presents Amoret's torture, Spenser directly identifies our psychological experience with the process of reading. Subordinate clauses and exclamations intervene between the major grammatical elements, "a wide wound," and "was to be seene"; each is a separate unit that presents a single aspect of a multiple response to Amoret's wound. The strikingly simple last line emerges from a context of deliberate confusions with which Spenser draws us in more closely.[5]

[5] "Narrative and Rhetoric in The Faerie Queene," in Studies in English Literature, II (1962), 43–44.

To this should be added Spenser's insistence that the object of desire, when considered as an object, must be treated cruelly. There is no woman here, only a breast; that is the emblem and the participant in the masque, and the central activity of the procession is the plunging of the knife in this stanza and the drawing forth of Amoret's heart in the next:

> At that wide orifice her trembling hart
> Was drawne forth, and in silver basin layd,
> Quite through transfixed with a deadly dart,
> And in her blood yet steeming fresh embayd . . .
>
> (III,xii,21)

The verbs are active, this is an event happening in the stanza, yet there is no visible agent. This focuses climactically all the wounds of love in the entire book and shows, more clearly than ever before, the way desire is in itself sadistic and, worse, dehumanizing. We cannot say that Cupid or Busirane or Cruelty is the "cruell hand" that despoils Amoret; the ultimate image of the assailant is not an image at all in the visual sense, just an action. It is hard to imagine anything more mysterious or chilling.

It is with something like relief that we then read of a human, if painfully tortured, Amoret:

> And those two villeins, which her steps upstayd,
> When her weake feete could scarcely her sustaine,
> And fading vitall powers gan to fade,
> Her forward still with torture did constraine,
> And evermore encreased her consuming paine.
>
> (III,xii,21)

Cruelty and Despight are only bullies, the Cupid that follows is only an imperious master, and in the next two

stanzas we have the final stages, the alternative for Amoret
in a world without Britomart:

> Behinde him was Reproch, Repentaunce, Shame;
> Reproch the first, Shame next, Repent behinde:
> Repentaunce feeble, sorowfull, and lame;
> Reproch despightful, carelesse, and unkinde;
> Shame most ill favourd, bestiall, and blinde:
> Shame lowrd, Repentaunce sigh'd, Reproch did
>   scould;
> Reproch sharpe stings, Repentaunce whips entwinde,
> Shame burning brond-yrons in her hand did hold:
> All three to each unlike, yet all made in one mould.
>
> (III,xii,24)

We have been here before, for this is only Malbecco after
the fire. But the abstractions make clear that this is not
now the story of an individual, but a statement of the
consequences of sexual desire—enfeeblement and self-
punishment. Following this comes chaos, expanded beyond the sexual: Strife, Care, Sorrow, Heavenly Venge-
aunce, Death with Infamy. No history could be more
relentless, austere, or devastating, yet it is all adequate to
a sense of experience perceivable by anyone.

But this ending is only an alternative and Britomart *is*
here, the central action still to come. She waits, "Nether
of ydle showes nor of false charmes aghast"; suddenly
what had been profoundly mysterious to Spenser and to
us is declared to be "ydle" and "false." At the end of her
waiting the door of the third room flies open, and there
is Amoret bound to a pillar and, for the first time, Busirane himself:

> And her before, the vile enchaunter sate,
> Figuring straunge characters of his art:
> With living blood he those characters wrate,

> *Dreadfully dropping from her dying hart,*
> *Seeming transfixed with a cruell dart;*
> *And all perforce to make her him to love.*
> *Ah! who can love the worker of her smart?*
>
> (III,xii,31)

This is the final metamorphosis of both Paridell and Cupid, the suitor seeking service and the master seeking dominance, welded together in an enchanter. Spenser cries, "Ah! who can love the worker of her smart?" as though such loving were impossible when in fact Book III is made up of those eager to love such a one. Even Britomart cannot escape completely; after she attacks Busirane he wounds her with the knife he seeks to plunge into Amoret:

> *Unwares it strooke into her snowie chest,*
> *That litle drops empurpled her faire brest.*
>
> (III,xii,33)

But Britomart is not Amoret, though she had experienced the experience of Amoret. She has been a passive maid, but also a knight, Chastity, a dispeller of rain and fire, and now she combines all these as romantic hero, magically endowed but mortal, facing the villain in the rescue of the heroine. To put it another way, Britomart *is* or *becomes* chastity by this combination of masculine hero and feminine wounded, of Cupid's mastery without his cruelty and Amoret's susceptibility without her weak passivity. Spenser's sense of the traditional materials of romance is so secure here that none of this kind of statement is needed in the poem; after all that has gone before, the action is enough.

Unfortunately, after Busirane is subdued Britomart does speak and is vastly inadequate to the experience:

> And to him said: 'Thou wicked man! whose meed
> For so huge mischiefe and vile villany
> Is death, or if that ought doe death exceed,
> Be sure that nought may save thee from to dy,
> But if that thou this dame doe presently
> Restore unto her health and former state;
> This doe and live, els dye undoubtedly.'
>
> (III,xii,35)

The last line is much the best; the rest is clogged and narrowing. But it is Spenser's first real lapse after one of the greatest of all sustained passages, and it is only a lapse, for in the next three stanzas we have what amounts to a brilliant encapsulation of the experience of the entire canto. First Busirane turns to his book:

> Full dreadfull thinges out of that balefull booke
> He red, and measur'd many a sad verse,
> That horrour gan the virgins hart to perse,
> And her faire locks up stared stiffe on end . . .
>
> (III,xii,36)

Then, as he undoes the enchantment the house quakes, the doors rattle, the pillar breaks:

> The cruell steele, which thrild her dying hart,
> Fell softly forth, as of his owne accord,
> And the wyde wound, which lately did dispart
> Her bleeding brest, and riven bowels gor'd,
> Was closed up, as it had not beene bor'd,
> And every part to safety full sownd,
> As she were never hurt, was soone restor'd:
> Tho, when she felt her selfe to be unbownd,
> And perfect hole, prostrate she fell unto the grownd.
>
> (III,xii,38)

To bide the burden of distress is to be heroic is to be made whole; the path that leads to Cupid's trophies and to Death with Infamy becomes the path of renewal: "As she were never hurt, was soone restor'd." The moment Spenser conceived of chastity as the supreme human achievement of sexual love both the hurt and the restoration were implicit. Here he faces and resolves the destructiveness of desire as earlier he faced and resolved, in the Garden, the destructiveness of decay. At the end of the cosmic vision is the mythic union of Venus and Adonis— "and of his sweetnesse takes her fill"; at the end of the romantic vision are the heroic fidelity of Britomart and the hermaphroditic union of Amoret and Scudamour:

> Lightly he clipt her twixt his armes twaine,
> And streightly did embrace her body bright,
> Her body, late the prison of sad paine,
> Now the sweet lodge of love and deare delight:
> But she, faire lady, overcommen quight
> Of huge affection, did in pleasure melt,
> And in sweete ravishment pourd out her spright:
> No word they spake, nor earthly thing they felt,
> But like two senceles stocks in long embracement
>   dwelt.
>
> (III,xii,45[1590])

They become one as Britomart has in herself combined hero and maid. As the blood came from her "fainting spright" when she was tortured, now Amoret herself "in sweete ravishment pourd out her spright." The body that had been her prison becomes the "sweet lodge of love" where both "dwell" in embracement.

To end this account of Book III with the version written in 1590 and later cancelled is not to deny that the real completion of Book III comes in Book IV. In the marriage of the Thames and the Medway and the return of Marinell and Florimell from the sea are combined the natural cosmos of the Garden of Adonis and the union of Amoret and Scudamour. But the advantage of using the cancelled version is that it emphasizes that the subject of Book III is not marriage but union—human, natural, and divine coming together. Not that the two are in any way disharmonious or even separate, but making the distinction does enable us to insist that Book III ends not with a sacrament but with an heroic rescue and a coming together. The possibility and even the ingredients for the sacrament are here right enough, but we are not yet ready. How hard to bring together, how destructive when separated—these are the major emphases.

Beyond that we do not need to go. It may be tempting to ask what is the "meaning" of the book as a whole, because taking one book at a time is one of the few available ways of organizing our sense of something so large and dense as this poem. But to take one book out of the poem, especially one so tied in with subsequent books, is to do it an injustice. Also, and much more important, if the account in this chapter has any appropriateness and validity, the meaning of a poem like *The Faerie Queene* is really only the journey we make through it. The organization and sense of world we create as we watch the sequence become completed are probably the most "meaning" it will ever have. In any attempt to render that sequence in commentary, falsifications are inevitable: selections must be made, emphases given, interpretations offered, and in an analysis as long as this a great deal is still left out. To compress "meaning" any further would be to settle for summary when journeys are what we need. Spenser was obviously delighted by what he could make of Faerie Land; the impression he gives throughout Book III, and for almost the whole poem, is primarily one of absorption. Whatever the advantages and shortcomings attendant upon this frame of mind, absorption on the part of the reader is almost inevitable if one is to read at all. This means that the more one looks at the poem and tries to be just to the art that made it, the more one's admiration grows for its predominant qualities—its brooding certainty, its compassion, its celebration of its own variety. Increasingly, then, it all seems to count and all about equally so that choosing one stanza to discuss at length and leaving others for summary seems a kind of violation of the very qualities one is admiring. All commentary makes the poem seem more intent on meaning something than the poem itself does. The critic points and says, "Look there," because he cannot do otherwise; but that is what *The Faerie Queene* does only rarely. Thus this account of Book III, long though it is, seems to me already narrowing enough and much more in need of expansion than compression into more emphatic statement.

To speak this way is to move in the direction of a good deal of recent criticism of the poem, though inevitably my interpretation varies from that of others. The kind of allegorical interpretation that once was popular is slowly being discredited precisely because it was so unjust and narrowing to Spenser's capaciousness. But still it seems to me that the tendency of even recent criticism is to be more emphatic, more concerned than Spenser is with a few things in the poem only. Here is a good example of the kind of commentary I mean:

The Adonis theme is represented in the male knights, all of whom are wounded. Timias' story renders the

theme in erotic terms. Since he forgoes woman's love
for Arthur, he does not follow Florimell, but pursues
instead the lustful Foster. Like Adonis who leaves
Venus for the boar hunt, he is wounded in the left
thigh by the Foster's 'bore-speare' . . .[6]

Mr. Hamilton then quotes the passage cited earlier:

> His locks, like faded leaves fallen to grownd,
> Knotted with blood in bounches rudely ran;
> And his sweete lips, on which before that stownd
> The bud of youth to blossome faire began,
> Spoild of their rosy red, were woxen pale and wan.
>
> (III,v,29)

My comment on the passage was that here, for the first
time in Book III, a victim is not alone and relief is soon
at hand. Mr. Hamilton's is rather different:

> The imagery of these lines links him with the god of
> nature. Only his 'sinfull wounds' (III,v,35) are not
> tended by Venus—here is Spenser's significant adapta-
> tion of the myth—but by the chaste Belphoebe. She
> cures only to wound again through love, and will not
> cure him by yielding the flower of her virginity.[7]

But the connections made here are really more tenuous
than Mr. Hamilton makes them seem. Timias is wounded
by a boar spear, Adonis by a boar. But the imagery
describing Adonis' fall is not really at all like the imagery
in Canto v:

[6] A. C. Hamilton, The Structure of Allegory in "The Faerie
Queene" (Oxford: Oxford University Press, 1961), pp. 140–
141.
[7] Ibid., p. 141.

Lo! where beyond he lyeth languishing,
Deadly engored of a great wilde bore,
And by his side the goddesse groveling
Makes for him endlesse mone, and evermore
With her soft garment wipes away the gore,
Which staynes his snowy skin with hatefull hew . . .

(III,i,38)

The whole sense of the passages is different; the one in Canto i is really about Venus who had tried to hide Adonis from his fate, while the one in Canto v is really about the wounded lad, a pathetic and lovely bud of youth. What is the connection, what are we to make of it? Mr. Hamilton goes on to mention other wounded figures: Marinell, Arthur, the Witch's son, the Squire of Dames, the Fisherman, Proteus, Malbecco, Paridell. But to do this is to wipe out any connections there might be between the wounded Adonis and the wounded Timias, and the moment we consider any male figure wounded by boars, foresters, or Cupid, we might as well include Brito-mart, Malecasta, and Amoret.

Mr. Hamilton is clearly aware of the dangers of as-signing meanings to these stories so as to bring them into some kind of allegorical lock step. But all we really have is the asserted link between Timias and Adonis, and another, not quite as clear, between Marinell and Adonis. Each connection, furthermore, tends to blur or distort the individual passages. Scaffolding is created and then left, a structure that articulates only itself. Something is lost, I am convinced, in such a procedure; not a "meaning" really, but the quality of Spenser's verse. The meaning in Mr. Hamilton's sense lies in the links and the con-nections, and anyone who has read thus far is quite aware that I have made many links and connections. But it will be noticed that Mr. Hamilton links two events that are almost two thousand lines apart and Spenser has done nothing more than create similar incidents to help us make the link. The best connections, as I have noted a number of times before, are those made from stanza to stanza. The passage above in Canto i is really best linked with the succeeding stanzas: Venus is wounded by love, tries to hold Adonis in secrecy, and she fails. Then comes the scene between Malecasta and Britomart, and the way the stanzas are linked here is perfectly clear. In Canto v, however, Timias is central as Adonis is not in Canto i. He is felled after a long battle, he lives with renowne, "thou gentlest squire alive," and then is movingly nursed to life by Belphoebe. To say this, of course, is only to summarize the action of the cantos. Yet it is precisely this action which is most important always, for without a strong sense of its sequence we are free to make any connection we please, and a great many people have done so with nothing like Mr. Hamilton's skill. Yet it seems to me even he has done both passages in question an injustice. The effort to bring together, to hold together in a structure of image or of abstraction is being done by Spenser in his way, and our way should be to adhere to his as closely as possible.

But this does not mean that no critical assessment should be attempted. Having read, having attempted to describe what we have seen, we are then free to evaluate the results. In one sense the judgment is implicit in everything the critic writes about his work at hand, and if a critic cannot write as well as his author, he must try. But more can be said. Many readers, having finished the poem, find Book III the finest of the six. Whether or not one agrees with the judgment, the moment we can feel one part is better than another we can go on to ask

wherein lies its excellence and we can move from description to judgment. Here is a description by C. S. Lewis
that is in itself an implicit judgment:

> His work is one, a growing thing, like a tree; like the
> world-ash-tree itself, with branches reaching to heaven
> and roots to hell. It reaches up to the songs of angels
> or the vision of the New Jerusalem and admits among
> its shining ones the veiled image of God Himself: it
> reaches down to the fertile chaos beneath the Garden
> of Adonis and to the grotesque satyrs who protect Una
> or debauch Hellenore with equal truth to their nature.
> And between these two extremes comes all the multi-
> plicity of human life, transmuted but not falsified by
> the conventions of chivalrous romance. The 'great
> golden chain of Concord' has united the whole of his
> world. What he feels on one level, he feels on all.
> When the good and fair appear to him, the whole man
> responds; the satyrs gambol, the lances splinter, the
> shining ones rise up. There is a place for everything
> and everything is in its place. Nothing is repressed;
> nothing is insubordinate. To read him is to grow in
> mental health.[8]

This will not pass as disinterested criticism for two reasons. Its description is not really accurate and it lets the
description serve for praise. What is wrong with the
description is that it describes *The Faerie Queene* as
though it were one large world picture on a wall whereas,
in fact, its motions are linear like those of a ticker-tape.
Perhaps one could extract from the poem a vision like
the one Lewis describes here and argue that such a vision
was Spenser's as he was writing the poem. But the poem

[8] *The Allegory of Love* (Oxford: Oxford University Press, 1936),
p. 359.

is not like this—what Lewis calls "up" and "down" and "extremes" and "united" are all not only his own terms but contrary to Lewis' own experience of reading, as the passage cited earlier reveals.

But what is really wrong is that Lewis assumes that because "nothing is repressed" in Faerie Land, reading Spenser is therefore healthy. When the good and fair appear to Spenser, we may say, the whole man tries to respond but the result is sometimes rather mechanical— there are much better examples of automatic responses in other books, but the reconcilement of Guyon and Britomart in Canto i which leads to the apostrophe "O goodly usage of those antique tymes" can safely be described as a response in excess of the presented object. The fact, furthermore, that what Spenser feels on one level he feels on all is not in itself a blessing if all it leads to is long-windedness, and it may be a sign of Spenser's own personal "health" and not of his literary excellence. When Lewis speaks of "levels" he forgets it is he that is making those levels, not Spenser. We can say that Spenser moves from Belphoebe the mortal huntress to Belphoebe as emblematic of virginal chastity, that he moves from Malbecco the frightened husband to Malbecco as Gelosy, but Spenser gives no indication that he thinks he is moving in any way except forward in his poem. Here, for instance, are two stanzas describing the mastery of Cupid in Canto xi that move from the "level" of the divine to the "level" of the human:

> Ne did he spare (so cruell was the elfe)
> His owne deare mother, (ah! why should he so?)
> Ne did he spare sometime to pricke himselfe,
> That he might taste the sweet consuming woe,

Which he had wrought to many others moe.
But to declare the mournfull tragedyes,
And spoiles, wherewith he all the ground did strow,
More eath to number with how many eyes
High heven beholdes sad lovers nightly theeveryes.

Kings, queenes, lords, ladies, knights, and damsels
    gent
Were heap'd together with the vulgar sort,
And mingled with the raskall rablement,
Without respect of person or of port,
To shew Dan Cupids powre and great effort:
And round about, a border was entrayld
Of broken bowes and arrowes shivered short,
And a long bloody river through them rayld,
So lively and so like that living sence it fayld.

                    (III,xi,45–46)

There are "levels" here as part of the subject—kings belong on a higher level than the "raskall rablement." But of course the point is that Cupid is destroying these levels. More important is the motion of the two stanzas which has nothing to do with levels, really. It begins with a wondering cry at Cupid's wounding of Venus, then goes to the god himself who, like everyone else, seeks to "taste the sweet consuming woe." The effect of this is to create the importance of Venus and Cupid only to destroy it; they too are leveled, they seek such leveling, and why should Cupid spare his mother? It is a staggering thought and leads to a dizzied sense of the immensity and completeness of Cupid's empire here; heaven does not have as many eyes to see as Cupid has slaves to make themselves sad with nightly thievery. He stops at kings and queens only to "heap" and "mingle" them with everyone else. Finally, we have the result of all this, the broken arrows and the river of blood. Differentiation, hierarchy, living things have been obliterated. The image is so "lively," so like life—both so "true" and so "dehumanized" that the senses fail to contemplate it.

Now this is not, by general consent, one of the supreme moments in the poem, but is like what takes place all the time. Yet the moment we begin to take in its careful fluidity, its participation in the inevitable and endless movement of the poem, we have begun to see how we should praise an undramatic writer. The stanzas look so placid and *are* placid, they are all alike but always shimmering, defining and redefining, so that the dominant sense is one of simultaneous lostness and foundness. The last four lines of the first stanza quoted above—"But to declare . . ." etc.—seem at first glance like mere filler, but at some point, either in the alexandrine or the beginning of the next stanza, we see what they are doing, dissolving the "scene" because that is what Cupid does. Yet this is as nothing compared to the splendor of the last four lines of the next stanza which really almost do what poems are sometimes vaguely said to do: create images so powerful that they can barely be contemplated. The action of these two stanzas alone is the action of quite a few novels when stripped of their sense of dramatic change and left only with the undramatic longing for the "sweet consuming woe" that leads inevitably to the river and the broken arrows. Yet these are only two stanzas, eighteen lines in a poem of many thousands.

Our trouble with such a poet seems to be that he has no problems. He does not, to use one of our usual terms of praise, face up to anything. It is this quality that makes him seem simple perhaps. But we can come closer to praising him rightly if we use the language of Dr. Leavis describing Wordsworth:

> What he had for presentment was a type and a stand-
> ard of human normality, a way of life; his preoccupa-
> tion with sanity and spontaneity working at a level
> and in a spirit it seems appropriate to call religious.[9]

Wordsworth comes later, after many changes in history of which Spenser could know nothing. Thus Wordsworth deals with his own life, presenting it as a "standard of human normality," and Spenser, more anonymous and therefore more secure in his impersonality, never quite impresses us that way. But the hallmarks of Spenser are here: sanity, spontaneity, human normality, conceived in a spirit of wonder that of course is "appropriate to call religious." To use another phrase of Leavis' about Words-worth: "He had, if not a philosophy, a wisdom to com-municate." The wisdom of Book III concerns love, the human uncertainty and want, the human heroic response to the loneliness of passion, the cosmological and divine reply and fulfillment. Of all the virtues it is the one that seems to have set Spenser freest because it could be more fully related to his sense of what life was like, more closely and densely allied with its deepest pains and most soaring achievements.

When we compare the third book with the better known first two, we can see differences in favor of Book III. Spenser always had enough conventional imagery, knowledge, and wisdom to keep him inventing, but in a poem of almost unbroken evenness the one thing that can really hurt are episodes or series of episodes that exist

---

[9] *Revaluation* (London: Chatto and Windus, 1936), p. 164.

only to set up a later episode. In Book I, for instance, Spenser has the Red Crosse Knight fight the dragon Error and two paynim knights, Sansloy and Sansfoy, in addition to the great dragon in Canto xi. The "point," we quickly see, is that the Red Crosse Knight defeats enemies known to be such, and falls victim to those more carefully hidden: Archimago, Duessa, Despair. Because the emphasis in the book is on the spiritual lot of men, which will include his liability to sin and error and his possible salvation, what absorbs Spenser most and frees him most are the hidden enemies and those figures of human and divine grace who help rescue the Knight in his moments of greatest peril. This means that the external enemies are not really relevant and that the point about them, once made, hardly needs elaboration. The paynim knights are extra and they badly clog the early cantos. In addition, the famed House of Pride, though able to stand sufficiently well as a set piece, does not really clarify the previous action as the set pieces so wonderfully do in Book III. Finally, the episode with Kirkrapine, Abessa, and Una in Canto iii is inept on any terms, standard mechanized allegory. All this means that Cantos ii–vi of Book I are only fitfully interesting, and the sequence itself generates little power. This becomes clearest, perhaps, when we see how magnificently Spenser handles what follows: the capture of the Red Crosse Knight treated in the previous chapter, the reappearance of Una, the appearance of Arthur, the exiling of Duessa, the trips to Despair and the House of Holiness. Here everything moves with great majesty: Una speaks to the Knight's plight in describing her own, Arthur speaks to the plight of the Knight, Una, and everyone. The sequence thus gathers great cumulative energy, so that when Spenser breaks in, at the opening of Canto ix: "O goodly golden chayne! wherewith yfere The vertues linked are in lovely wize," we have a moment of definition and redefinition like those that stud the later cantos of Book III. It focuses for us the disasters of Cantos vii–viii, it begins to show a way out of the prison of Orgoglio, yet it does not deny that the Giant Despair still lies ahead.

Spenser cannot always rely, then, on his ability to write occasionally stunning passages; he needs his sequence, because that is, finally, his vision and his sense of existence. "This is the way to see" is the implicit gesture made by the poem, but it can really be made only as the sequence keeps showing us a "this" and then another "this" which illuminates and relights the first "this." In Book I, it seems to me, what Spenser really sees is in the last six cantos. But in Book III almost everything counts, fits, is made relevant the moment we read it. One can see blemishes: the clumsiness at the beginning of the first canto, the fight with the foresters at the beginning of the fifth, perhaps the grisly comedy by the seashore in Cantos vii–viii. But these are only blemishes. What is most distinctive about Book III as a whole, above and beyond the few excerptible moments of greatness, is the magnificence of the modulations, the shifts in tone, temper, plane. The pain and joy of love allow Spenser to show, over and over and in many shifting ways, the relation between one thing and another. Sometimes the relation is between a character and the larger universe, as in the episodes in Canto iv; here we see the relationship within a line or stanza, locally. Sometimes the relation is between the pain of love leading to chastity and the pain leading to viciousness; here the relationship is

made over a series of cantos, most obviously those surrounding the Garden of Adonis where the allegorical
focus provided by the Garden reilluminates the experience of Britomart and Timias and also, as we come on
them, shows us how to read about the passions of the
witch's son, Argante, the fisherman, and Proteus. Sometimes the relation is among various forms of the same
essence, as with the reworkings of the tapestries of Canto
xi in the Maske of Cupid in Canto xii or with the re-
workings of Paridell's need to own in Malbecco; in these
instances the work is done by close juxtaposition and a
repetition of phrase and image. But this establishing of
relationships does more than simply create a sense of
great denseness, though that is much. They also are so
made that they can set off the unique and momentarily
unrelated, a character or an attitude seen as for the first
time. The nursing of Timias, as we have seen, gains its
quality of touching care and tenderness because it comes
after a long series of failures. The heroism of Britomart is
created almost entirely by Spenser's keeping her apart
from the figures in the tapestries and the Maske. What
she actually does with Busirane and Amoret is really very
little; read by itself the episode is only a dozen stanzas
about three rather indistinct characters. But because
Britomart is breaking into such a long chain of dominated
lovers and their masters she seems spectacular. Such too
is the case with the unraveling of her hair in Canto ix.
Throughout the book the sense of sequence is superb,
and the test of this is the way so many passages of good
but not overwhelming poetry take on life because of their
placement. Perhaps the finest single example of this is
Britomart's speech to Scudamour outside Busirane's castle.
Because nothing in *The Faerie Queene* is separated from

the rest and thus made to seem important as a self-sustained passage, this is not a speech that will ever stand beside Cleopatra's dream of an Emperor Antony or Macbeth's response to the news of his wife's death. But because it is the first human reply to the pain of human love it assumes a stature in its context that not only makes it heroic in itself, but that alters our response to all that follows. These relationships, this establishment of sequence, is of course a matter of artistic mastery, but the mastery is only superficially a matter of technique. It is the result of Spenser's knowledge, its density and security combined with his constant sense of wonder. He does not make one believe he knows because he has mastered a system or a peculiar way of writing poetry, but because he has seen and understood the roles of human feeling and action within his received universe. Everything is in its place—yes, but it is the richness of his sense of "place" and the awe engendered by that richness that is the achievement of Book III.

The wisdom of Spenser—it should not be an embarrassing phrase. Not the wisdom of an aphorist or of a philosophic thinker, but of a visionary of the ordinary world. Faerie is simply his means of illuminating what— it sometimes seems—everyone else has seen imperfectly. The growth that is fulfillment is in the Garden of Adonis, yet while we are on the plain we seldom remember this. Spenser honors both facts, the growth and the forgetfulness, by celebrating the one and by being generous and compassionate with the other. The poem goes on and on, not because Spenser can do this but because he must do this in order to be clear in that full way that is the sign of his seeing. But this, which is most true in Book III and always true in a general way throughout the first four books, did not go on forever. There came a time when Spenser looked at things he could not or could no longer transform into Faerie, and the moment that happened the future of the poem was doomed. To that moment we must now turn.

IV   *What Happened to*

The

Faerie Queene

*B*ooks IV–VI were published in 1596, but almost certainly they were finished some time earlier. In the eightieth sonnet of the *Amoretti*, written in 1594, Spenser writes:

> *After so long a race as I have run*
> *Through Faery Land, which those six books compile,*
> *Give leave to rest me, being halfe fordonne,*
> *And gather to my selfe new breath awhile.*

If Spenser is not exaggerating he had completed these three books, a matter of more than fifteen thousand lines, in less than four years. But a good deal had in fact been written earlier, perhaps as long before as 1580 when *The Faerie Queene* was still nebulous to Spenser. Book

IV is a continuation of Book III, and its designs and many of its episodes were probably finished when the first three books were published. It belongs, in spirit, design, and even execution, to the 1580's. So too does some of Book V: the marriage of Florimell, the central episodes with Radigund, the simple exempla of justice. But the remainder of Book V, including the long stretch of historical allegory at the end, plus Book VI, belongs to the period 1591–1594.

In all three books of the second installment there are signs of hasty composition and assembling. Some incidents—the uniting of Amyas, Placidas and their ladies in IV,ix, the meeting of the six knights and the reunion of Scudamour and Amoret in the same canto, the tournament at Florimell's wedding in V,iii—Spenser tells without concealing his lack of interest in the proceedings. Also, there are many lines Spenser would have rewritten had he reread them, such as these:

> That she uneath discerned, whether whether weare.
>> (IV,ix,10)

> 'The whilest their eldest brother was away,
> Cupid, their eldest brother . . .'
>> (IV,x,42)

> 'Leave, faytor, quickely that misgotten weft
> To him that hath it better justifyde . . .'
>> (VI,i,18)

There is also a sharp increase in feminine rhymes, and these involve Spenser in a kind of verbal humor, some of which is almost certainly unintended and almost all of which bespeaks a lack of absorption in the material; this can also be seen in the increased use of the authorial "I," announcements about the closing of cantos à la Ariosto, and in the bitter outburst in IV,viii,29 about the "misregard" of some "rash witted wight" for his poetry.

This evidence can be interpreted in a number of ways. The simplest and maybe the best way is to note, first, that most of the real carelessness is in Book IV, and second, that the parts undoubtedly written after 1590 all show that something "has happened" to the poem. It would appear that Spenser, when he returned to Ireland in 1591, hurried through those parts of the poem which had already been written, reworking and stitching offhandedly, so he might then get on with what was most pressing to him then. Book IV, thus, can be seen as chock full of blemishes and flaws but also as a work whose design is sound, even bold. This is not the place for a long look at Book IV, but it can be said that no book that so beautifully places and renders the meeting of Britomart and Artegall discussed in the second chapter above, or that moves so assuredly near the end—from the Temple of Venus through the marriage of the Thames and Medway to the reunion of Florimell and Marinell—is really different from Books I–III. Spenser may not have been working very hard to make it all go smoothly, but he was working with material that at some time he had seen as clearly and carefully as he saw anything in the poem.

But the last two books *are* different, and that difference is announced at the very beginning of Book V. The proem here is at once the longest, least decorative, and most revealing of the six prologues:

> So oft as I with state of present time
> The image of the antique world compare,
> When as mans age was in his freshest prime,
> And the first blossome of faire vertue bare,

Such oddes I finde twixt those, and these which are,
As that, through long continuance of his course,
Me seemes the world is runne quite out of square
From the first point of his appointed sourse,
And being once amisse, growes daily wourse and
  wourse.

(V,1)

Spenser praises the antique world many times before this, but never so exclusively and narrowly at the expense of the present. He has never so thoroughly condemned the present, for instance, that he could not easily transform it into the time of Gloriana. But here he offers not only a contrast but a definition of historical motion that means that nothing now could ever be right or set right again. Here is a voice that argued the same way earlier in the poem:

'*For he that once hath missed the right way,*
The further he doth goe, the further he doth stray.'

(I,ix,43)

But the name of that voice is Despair and Spenser then had carefully dissociated himself from it; here he adopts Despair's very accent, and then goes on:

For that which all men then did vertue call
Is now cald vice; and that which vice was hight,
Is now hight vertue, and so us'd of all . . .

(V,4)

This is clearly no preliminary embellishment, yet the more seriously he means it the more genuinely his whole enterprise is threatened. If what he and the antique world call virtue is now called vice, then the effort which aims to envision a universe in which we all live is no longer worth making, and the attempt to fashion a gentleman in a romance has been reduced to a lyric cry. For Spenser, to lose his assured sense of his relationship with his audience is to lose everything. His names must be our names, his virtue our virtue and his vice our vice, or else his whole evocative power has been cramped and compromised. As Harry Berger, whose treatment of the shift being noted here is much the best to date, has said:

> The fragmented and chaotic appearance of the present challenges the antique vision of order. . . . History does not reveal progress, or reason, or a divine plan; only the relics of decay, fallen civilization, time and elde.[1]

The dourness expressed here in the proem to Book V is something new, marring, and troubling; beneath it is a resentment and an impulse to satire that can only alter the bearings of a poem like *The Faerie Queene*. It is tempting to explain this shift by saying it is only the result of shifting from the private to the public virtues, but the argument is a weak one and can be destroyed from two distinct points of view, both of which offer us a better chance to see what has happened to Spenser and his poem.

To say that Holiness, Temperance, and Chastity are private virtues and that Friendship, Justice, and Courtesy are more social is to make a distinction which, before Book V, the poem never allows for. When Timias, for instance, is wounded deep in a forest in Book III, he

---

[1] "The Prospect of Imagination," *Studies in English Literature,* I (1961), 98–99.

nonetheless "lives with renowne" because he has fought courageously. Given our usual distinctions, this is absurd because if there is no one around to know how he has fought, then there is no one to give him the renown Spenser says he merits. But Spenser knows no such distinctions: fame and the acts which create fame are one. When Britomart attacks Busirane, we are dealing simultaneously with an external "social" event and a private occurrence in the heart, though no one would ever put the matter this way without being compelled to do so. So too, in those episodes in Book V probably written before 1590, Spenser handles justice without making any clear distinction between "public" and "private." Here, for instance, is part of Britomart's dream in the Temple of Isis:

> Tho turning all his [the crocodile's] pride to humblesse
>   meeke,
> Him selfe before her [Britomart's] feete he lowly
>   threw,
> And gan for grace and love of her to seeke:
> Which she accepting, he so neare her drew,
> That of his game she soone enwombed grew,
> And forth did bring a lion of great might;
> That shortly did all other beasts subdew.
>
> (V,vii,16)

The last two lines allow for our seeing the union of maid and crocodile politically; the lion that is their issue has great might and "did all other beasts subdew." But it allows for this without for a moment denying the private erotic dream. If forced to interpret the passage allegorically we might say: "The union of Britomart and Artegall establishes political equity in the realm." But, of course, to say that would be to lose the sense of the sequence of "seeke," "accept," "game," and "enwombed" that is the stanza's central action. We can notice that the priest, when he comes to gloss the dream for Britomart, does not make of it simple allegory, or vast public event:

> 'Then shalt thou take him to thy loved fere,
> And joyne in equall portion of thy realme:
> And afterwards a sonne to him shalt beare,
> That lion-like shall shew his powre extreame.'
>
> (V,vii,23)

The sexual act is here a joining "in equall portion of thy realme," but "realme" is both Britomart and Britomart's kingdom; the lion is now a "lion-like" son, but is neither more nor less "public" than he was in the dream itself. Spenser's vision here is as securely one as it is anywhere in the poem, and the moment we ask of it that it be public or private or even "both at once" we have put a strain on the passage it obviously should not be asked to bear. In the context of the whole episode, both erotic dream and political union are "there" securely.

But this may seem like a special case because the experience in the Temple does not deal with justice directly. Spenser had, however, many other ways available to him of rendering his virtue that would also keep him strictly within the confines of the poem he had been writing. Indeed there is perhaps no greater institution anywhere for dissolving potential distinctions between public and private than the English Common Law and its courts, where the "public" law is only the collective "private" experience of the people. Spenser's poem and the Common Law both seek by means of great flexibility to be fully responsive to the immediate particular case and to some dimly seen but fully felt ideal. Neither moves simply from the particular to the abstract but instead constantly modulates between the two. One could write very responsively for a long time about *The Faerie Queene* by using two terms, "facts" and "appeal," strictly as they are used in the courts, for both poem and law are marked by an easy comprehensiveness and lack of codification. The system that could devise Wrongful Death as grounds for a civil suit and that could be so fully responsive to contingencies as to invent the Case of the Fertile Octogenarian is obviously one Spenser could have transformed into Faerie. Indeed, the palmer in the Bower of Bliss and Britomart when speaking to Scudamour before Busirane's castle are both Common Law judges.

That Spenser did not do this or anything like this is not the result, then, of any obduracy in his material, but rather the result of Spenser's own shift in interest and intent. The most obvious sign of something new is the presence of Talus, Artegall's one-man police force. A rendering of justice along the lines of the model Common Law accepts the common ideals on which that law and Spenser's poem are based. But the proem to Book V shows that Spenser no longer felt that common bond that had hitherto made him pale. In the world what he called "right" was now called "wrong," and so his sense of justice became his indignant sense of the wrong around him; Talus is his instrument for administering right in an alien world. Along with Talus is something else new in the poem: the constant presence of a faceless and lawless multitude. Spenser had put his enemies into Faerie Land, as it were, and has responded to them with Talus, "made of yron mould, Immoveable, resistlesse, without end." His task is simply destructive—he routs, he lays waste, he "thresht out falshood, and did truth unfould." The result is a willed sadism that would have been imaginable earlier only if the torturer were a Busirane:

> Yet for no pitty would he change the cours
> Of justice, which in Talus hand did lye;
> Who rudely hayld her forth without remorse,
> Still holding up her suppliant hands on hye,
> And kneeling at his feete submissively.
> But he her suppliant hands, those hands of gold,
> And eke her feete, those feete of silver trye,
> Which sought unrighteousnesse, and justice sold,
> Chopt off, and nayld on high, that all might
>   them behold.
>
> (V,ii,26)

There is nothing careless here; sad to say, the verse enacts Spenser's purposes fully. After the second mention of Munera's suppliant hands Spenser builds up his stanza with two and a half lines of subordinate phrases so as to come down strongly in the alexandrine on those hands, "Chopt off, and nayld on high, that all might them behold." The stanza moves with the motions of Talus' guillotine-like blows, and we end with the first of many tokens of Talus' presence, the hands nailed as fulfillment and as threat.

To show how darkly the clouds are gathering over Spenser here we need only compare this with another stanza of destruction. In the Bower of Bliss, after a beautifully sustained passage describing Verdant asleep in Acrasia's arms while a voice sings "Gather the rose of love, whilest yet is time," Guyon moves in, and what he does is explicitly destructive and so implicitly wrong:

> But all those pleasant bowres and pallace brave
> Guyon broke downe, with rigour pittilesse;
> Ne ought their goodly workmanship might save
> Them from the tempest of his wrathfulnesse,
> But that their blisse he turn'd to balefulnesse:
> Their groves he feld, their gardins did deface,
> Their arbers spoyle, their cabinets suppresse,
> Their banket houses burne, their buildings race,
> And, of the fayrest late, now made the fowlest place.
>
> (II,xii,83)

The Bower is consistently a "good" place—"blisse," "fayrest," "pleasaunt bowres," "pallace brave," and "goodly workmanship" are the phrases—and Guyon is consistently rude and savage. But in Book V the savagery is implicitly praised by having it oppose "unrighteousnesse," so that Talus is not seen as cruel but as fulfilling "the cours Of justice." Even more telling is the way Spenser places these stanzas by means of the ones that follow. Guyon's assault leads into the palmer's "temperate" response. He transforms the beasts into their original shapes as men, then magnificently judges and releases the one who seeks to remain bestial: " 'Let Gryll be Gryll, and have his hoggish minde.' " In this way Guyon's destructiveness is placed as a type of puritanical wantonness, as intemperate in its way as Acrasia is in hers. The stanzas which follow Talus' slaughter of Lady Munera, however, only describe more maiming in the name of justice, and the episode is followed by the one with the egalitarian giant who is rebuked, and then he too is summarily disposed of: "And down the rock him throwing, in the sea him dround."

Spenser spent his mature years in Ireland trying to enforce a ruthless and alien English rule there, and the need expressed here to stamp out "injustice" in ways that recall the Final Solution undoubtedly reflects his frustration and anger with the world he saw around him. Justice is for him here a matter of suppression, administration, and foreign policy, the desperate expedient of one who feels betrayed by the world and no longer has any faith in legal redress. Artegall has no need to judge Pollente and Munera because he knows the right beforehand. It is not until closer to the end of Book V, however, that we see the real implications of what has happened: in Cantos viii–xii justice is prophetic history, written at a time when prophecy had become for Spenser what it was for William Blake all his life: a cry of pain in an indifferent and chaotic world. Spenser had brought contemporary history into his poem before without marring its serenity—the Kirkrapine episode in Book I is handled very mechanically but is only a local lapse, and the Timias-Belphoebe episodes in Books III–IV with their rendering of the affair between Raleigh and Elizabeth are very deftly handled, so that we can read in the contemporary allusions or not just as we wish. But by the early 1590's this simple accommodation of history was no longer possible for him. The last five cantos of Book V attempt a large-scale reworking of contemporary events, but the result is that Faerie Land only mirrors political and military events instead of illuminating them. There has been a good deal of disagreement about the precise references made in these cantos, but on the following almost everyone is in agreement:

Canto viii	Arthur defeats Soldan	*The defeat of the Spanish Armada* (1588)
Canto ix	Duessa's trial	*Imprisonment and execution of Mary, Queen of Scots* (1569–1587)

Canto x	Arthur rescues Lady Belgee	*Leicester's expedition to the Netherlands* (1586)
Canto xi	Arthur defeats Gerioneo	*Battle of Zutphen* (1586)
	Artegall and Burbon	*England helps Henry IV of France* (1593–1594)
Canto xii	Artegall defeats Grantorto and frees Irena	*Lord Grey in Ireland* (1580–1582)

We can notice two facts about Spenser's vision of history right away: 1) Catholicism is always the enemy, and 2) facts are distorted and often rearranged. What Spenser envisions is a rising tide of Protestant English strength, and so he makes things happen that did not happen—Arthur's defeat of Gerioneo as an account of Leicester's disastrous expedition in the Netherlands—or that only partly happened—Artegall's defeat of Grantorto in the Salvage Island—or that in fact happened but are not the victories Spenser imagined—Mercilla's execution of Duessa. In all but one instance Arthur and Artegall are simply administrators of a preordained foreign policy. In fighting the Soldan, Gerioneo, and Grantorto, Arthur and Artegall only fight because their enemies are only enemies. Because the moral valences are fixed there can be no surprises, and so Spenser must rely on brute narrative inventiveness to keep the action moving. Because this was never his strength as a poet, these cantos are like what Spenser's detractors claim the whole poem is like: a series of thudding, moralizing stanzas.

But were these cantos only a dull stretch of allegorized history, Spenser might well have moved on from them to great things, and indeed this is the usually accepted way of interpreting these cantos. But if the proem to Book V,

if the ominous presence of Talus early in the book, if
the ruthless treatment of mobs were not enough, then the
one episode in these last five cantos that is not a simple
matter of fighting bad people would show us that much
more was in fact at stake for Spenser and his poem than
a momentary lapse. In the Castle of Mercilla we have
Spenser's most determined effort to show that his vision
of justice is not simply a strenuous exercise in the wield-
ing of power. In Canto ix Arthur and Artegall come to
the castle and there they see Mercilla "Dealing of justice
with indifferent grace." Soon comes "The tryall of a great
and weightie case," and Duessa appears:

> Then was there brought, as prisoner to the barre,
> A ladie of great countenance and place,
> But that she it with foule abuse did marre;
> Yet did appeare rare beautie in her face,
> But blotted with condition vile and base,
> That all her other honour did obscure,
> And titles of nobilitie deface:
> Yet in that wretched semblant, she did sure
> The peoples great compassion unto her allure.
>
> (V,ix,38)

This is no simple enacting of predetermined right:
"abuse," vile blots, and obscured honor are balanced by
"great countenance and place," "rare beautie," and
wretchedness that stirs compassion in the people. During
the trial Spenser continues to balance the harsh judgment
against Duessa with a strong sense of her command of
sure grounds for mercy: Zele, Religion, Peoples Cry, and
Justice speak out against her while Pittie, Regard of
Womanhead, Daunger, and Griefe defend her. At this
point Artegall is against mercy and Arthur is for it. Then
Zele shifts the argument and parades Duessa's private

vices—Murder, Incontinence of Lyfe, Adulterie, Impietie
—and Arthur is swayed. The scene is beautifully set up
so that Duessa's guilt is not in question but that the
claims for compassion are nonetheless strong. So all turn
to Mercilla, seated high above, for her decree:

> But she, whose princely breast was touched nere
> With piteous ruth of her so wretched plight,
> Though plaine she saw, by all that she did heare,
> That she of death was guiltie found by right,
> Yet would not let just vengeance on her light;
> But rather let in stead thereof to fall
> Few perling drops from her faire lampes of light;
> The which she covering with her purple pall
> Would have the passion hid, and up arose withall.
>
> (V,ix,50)

Here, suddenly and inexplicably, the canto stops.

Mary, Queen of Scots had been effectively captured in
1569 and for the next eighteen years Elizabeth had
tempered the cries of her citizens for Mary's head by
letting her live, even though Mary was a magnet for all
dissidents who would restore Catholicism in England.
The case against Mary was very strong and urged by
Elizabeth's most powerful advisors, yet Elizabeth both
acknowledged their arguments and refused to act upon
them; Mary was guilty but there were many reasons why
she should not be executed. It must have seemed to Spenser like a perfect example of political mercy extended by
a master politician. But it was not, and nothing shows
this more clearly than the tell-tale break at the end of
Canto ix:

> The which she covering with her purple pall
> Would have the passion hid, and up arose withall.

CANTO X
Prince Arthur takes the enterprize
For Belgee for to fight:
Gerioneos seneschall
He slayes in Belges right.

Some clarkes doe doubt in their devicefull art,
Whether this heavenly thing whereof I treat,
To weeten Mercie, be of Justice part,
Or drawne forth from her by divine extreate.
This well I wote, that sure she is as great,
And meriteth to have as high a place,
Sith in th' Almighties everlasting seat
She first was bred, and borne of heavenly race;
From thence pour'd down on men, by influence of
grace.

(V,ix,50–x,1)

For anyone who has felt the impress of the poem to this point, the break is very moving. Mercilla rises, and in the introductory quatrain Spenser acts as though the episode were over and he could move easily on to Arthur's journey to Belgee. Then, fussily, fraudulently, but very touchingly, Spenser actually scurries around his subject. The obvious question left at the end of the ninth canto is, "What is merciful about Mercilla," and the opening stanza of the next canto shows that Spenser cannot answer the question and so he throws in a rhetorical smokescreen about the divine origin of mercy.

What *is* merciful about Mercilla? After two more distracting stanzas, we find out:

Much more it praysed was of those two knights,
The noble Prince and righteous Artegall,
When they had seene and heard her doome a rights

> *Against Duessa, damned by them all;*
> *But by her tempred without griefe or gall,*
> *Till strong constraint did her thereto enforce:*
> *And yet even then ruing her wilfull fall*
> *With more then needfull naturall remorse,*
> *And yeelding the last honour to her wretched corse.*
>
> (V,x,4)

It takes a number of readings before one realizes that
the sixth line here says Duessa is executed, and the ob-
scurity reveals Spenser's unwillingness to describe this
simple unmerciful "mercy." Elizabeth finally ordered
Mary's head chopped off, in which act there was nothing
merciful except perhaps the regret with which it was
done. So Spenser adds "And yet even then . . ." But
the poem has split here. Elizabeth was merciful, perhaps,
to Mary, but Mercilla only weeps over Duessa and then
has "strong constraint . . . her thereto enforce." Looking
at the historical event we can see that what was merciful
was the hesitancy and temporizing, the eighteen years of
respite between judgment and execution. But in the time-
less sequence such a space of time takes no longer to
pass than it does to say the words that name its duration:
in this poem, eighteen years could only be three syllables.
That Spenser at least partially realized what he had done
is shown in the sharp breaking off of the ninth canto.
He had never before reached a point where he could not
go on and write the fifty-first or fifty-second stanza—it is
precisely the freedom of the undramatic writer, as we have
seen, that he can so continue to move and name. Spenser,
locked into using Faerie Land as a means of rendering
history, suddenly betrays his medium. The point is not
that Mercilla had always to be merciful—Britomart is not
always chaste and the Red Crosse Knight is seldom holy—

but that what Mercilla does is something Spenser has to call merciful, has to insist is merciful, even though he has no way of rendering it as such. Mercilla and Spenser are both caught in history; when the split between the cantos comes we have the first dramatic moment in the poem.

Of course Spenser must act as though this were not so and, at least on the surface it would seem as if the break were only momentary. But everything else in Book V, both before and after this moment, shows that this is not the case. The consequences of conceding his Faerie Land to his prophetic history are much graver than a simple lapse. Make Talus both cruel and right, become strident with the fear of a lost audience, insist that Justice is primarily the administration of foreign policy, and the moral and therefore imaginative prices are bound to be higher than a momentary blurred vision in which execution is called merciful. Arthur goes to Belgee and defeats Gerioneo, Artegall tries to free Burbon from the masses and then crowns his career with the defeat of Grantorto and the freeing of Irena. The Protestant tide rises and history is still prophetic vision. But although the poem tries to maintain its patriotic vision, the press of historical events was too great, as the very end of the book makes so movingly clear. At the end of each of the previous books nothing is finally settled—Acrasia and Busirane are only two of the guises evil assumes. We do not expect tidiness such as we might find in a Shakespearean comedy or a Chaucerian tale. But even so, the end of Book V is shocking. After Artegall rescues Irena comes this:

> *Who streight her leading with meete majestie*
> *Unto the pallace, where their kings did rayne,*
> *Did her therein establish peaceablie,*

> *And to her kingdomes seat restore agayne;*
> *And all such persons as did late maintayne*
> *That tyrants part, with close or open ayde,*
> *He sorely punished with heavie payne;*
> *That in short space, whiles there with her he stayd,*
> *Not one was left that durst her once have disobayd.*
>
> (V,xii,25)

Thus far Spenser is able to go after the manner of the earlier books. But he cannot stop there because he is too absorbed in colonial administration to stop:

> *During which time that he did there remaine,*
> *His studie was true justice how to deale,*
> *And day and night employ'd his busie paine*
> *How to reforme that ragged common-weale:*
> *And that same yron man, which could reveale*
> *All hidden crimes, through all that realme he sent,*
> *To search out those that usd to rob and steale,*
> *Or did rebell gainst lawfull government;*
> *On whom he did inflict most grievous punishment.*
>
> (V,xii,26)

Justice "deals" with "busie paine" and so is synonymous with imperialism; Talus, thus, can torture the citizens of the Salvage Island and Artegall can inflict grievous punishment on them. It is awful that our serene and wondering poet should have been reduced to this.

But even here he cannot quite fail to acknowledge the wages of sin. Artegall is summoned inexplicably back to Faerie Court, and on his way home the hero reaps his reward:

> *Tho, as he backe returned from that land,*
> *And there arriv'd againe, whence forth he set,*

> *He had not passed farre upon the strand,*
> *When as two old ill favour'd hags he met,*
> *By the way side being together set;*
> *Two griesly creatures; and, to that their faces*
> *Most foule and filthie were, their garments yet,*
> *Being all rag'd and tatter'd, their disgraces*
> *Did much the more augment, and made most*
> *   ugly cases.*
>
> (V,xii,28)

Spenser's bitterness at the failure of his own factional causes cannot finally be checked. Prophetic vision gives way and Artegall is a ravenous wolf amongst scattered flocks of sheep, beset by curs:

> *Who when they nigh approching had espyde*
> *Sir Artegall, return'd from his late quest,*
> *They both arose, and at him loudly cryde,*
> *As it had bene two shepheards curres had scryde*
> *A ravenous wolfe amongst the scattered flocks.*
> *And Envie first, as she that first him eyde,*
> *Towardes him runs, and with rude flaring lockes*
> *About her eares, does beat her brest and forhead*
> *   knockes.*
>
> (V,xii,38)

Spenser is naked and alone now, powerless beside a powerless Artegall, near the end of his vision of history and near the end of everything. And so he gives us the Blatant Beast, his most terrifying vision of evil. He runs on, not an enemy to anything, not a recognized and defined foe as in different ways Busirane and Grantorto were. He is just the Blatant Beast:

> *Thereto the Blatant Beast, by them set on,*
> *At him began aloud to barke and bay,*
> *With bitter rage and fell contention,*
> *That all the woods and rockes nigh to that way*
> *Began to quake and tremble with dismay,*
> *And all the aire rebellowed againe,*
> *So dreadfully his hundred tongues did bray:*
> *And evermore those hags them selves did paine*
> *To sharpen him, and their owne cursed tongs did*
>   *straine.*

(V,xii,41)

Talus still believes he is in the old world of rigid justice,
and so wants to "chastize" the hags and the Blatant Beast.
But Artegall, like Spenser, knows that worse than giants
and monsters are in the world. He prevents Talus from
striking out and then moves on himself, leaving the
world to darkness, the hags, and the beast:

>   *yet he for nought would swerve*
> *From his right course, but still the way did hold*
> *To Faery court, where what him fell shall else be*
>   *told.*

(V,xii,43)

There the book ends, and whatever "else" was to be told
about Artegall, the knight in the magic glass of King
Ryence, the crocodile that protects and then makes love
to Britomart, is only a nostalgia now. Faerie Land has
collapsed, Spenser looks at the world around him and
shudders, and because he shudders he can no longer
describe what he sees in the terms he used to build his
vision and poem. All dramatic worlds are out of joint,
and the end of Book V is one of the origins of dramatic

literature. Faerie Land no longer exists as a viable way to describe the moral nature of action in a harmonious universe; it is now only part of a larger, fragmented, dramatic way of seeing.

It is tempting to attribute this collapse to Spenser's failure to win for himself the court position he had sought for so long, and to see his bitterness, thus, as the result of his realization when he returned to Ireland in 1591 that he would never leave that savage island again:

> The return to the 'lowly life', we may reasonably suspect, was forced upon the poet before being accepted by him; without the blasting of his 'idle hopes', the 'vainenesse' which he denounces in court life might well have seemed acceptable enough. Awakening, in other words, followed disappointment instead of preceding it . . .[2]

As far as it goes, this is probably true enough. But lest we conclude that Book V is simply the product of a decorating imagination become spiteful in the face of disaster, we should consider what was happening at the same time with other writers as sensitive as Spenser. We have seen that Spenser in some way locked himself into a way of seeing history as a linked linear chain:

> *Me seemes the world is runne quite out of square*
> *From the first point of his appointed sourse,*
> *And being once amisse, growes daily wourse and*
> *   wourse.*

(V,1)

---

[2] Derek Traversi, "The Faerie Queene," in *The Age of Chaucer*, Boris Ford, ed. (London: Penguin Books, 1954), p. 227.

This is a new vision of history both for himself and for
literature. The whole conception of Faerie Court, of
Gloriana and Arthur, or Merlin's vision of the rooted tree
of England, of Britomart's dream of herself as mother to
the lion—all this is based on the assumption that history
does not follow the principles of entropy, that restoration
and flowering are both possible and real. Almost all
literary visions of history before Book V of *The Faerie
Queene* are based on one of a number of conceptions of
cycles: the wheel of Fortune, the raising and lowering of
the buckets, the seeds of restoration planted in the ruins
of chaos. Shakespeare's first four history plays, for instance, written as Spenser was writing the second installment of his poem, describe an historical cycle that goes
from its presumed origins in the murder of Richard II
to the loss of order in England that is the War of the
Roses. Out of the war comes the ultimate horror, the un-
natural man Richard III, but from whom springs the
responding and restoring forces of Richmond and the
Tudor monarchy. Students of these plays know how
thoroughly this conception of history is grounded in many
Elizabethan chronicles and treatises. But in the second
group of four plays, *Richard II, Henry IV,* and *Henry V,*
Shakespeare dramatizes something quite different. He
pictures no golden age of the reign of Richard II but
rather an obscure enacting of the destruction of a magical
conception of kingship. This conception, once destroyed,
never returns. Hal's greatest achievements come in a
world far different from Richard II's, and he manages to
hold his world together by means of an heroic defeat of
Hotspur and a witty defeat of Falstaff; that he can both
kill Hotspur and concede the honor of that killing to
Falstaff allows him to destroy the rebel faction and to
render Falstaff speechless. But this achievement is pos-

sible only as a response to an historical moment, and when that moment passes, the best responses change too. Hal becomes weary in 2 *Henry IV*, Rumor runs rampant, Falstaff dominates because his voice responds most fully to the loss of possibility. Finally, in *Henry V*, with plump Jack banished and with him the world, we move into an iron age very similar to that of Book V of *The Faerie Queene*. The mystic presumption of divinity which illuminated Richard II and the detached triumph of Hal at Shrewesbury have both become merely past events, responses to earlier moments in time, and Henry V is left with having to forge a nation out of a jingoistic cry for foreign wars. The old relationship between king and kingdom enunciated in Gaunt's dying speech and in the Gardener's scene in *Richard II* is replaced with the forceful and cruel patriotism; the King now cries "if we be hind'red, We shall your tawny ground with your red blood Discolor":

> *The gates of mercy shall be all shut up,*
> *And the fleshed soldier, rough and hard of heart,*
> *In liberty of bloody hand shall range*
> *With conscience wide as hell, mowing like grass*
> *With fresh fair virgins and your flow'ring infants.*
>
> (*Henry V*, III,3,10–14)

That is the voice of Artegall and Talus, and, like theirs, its cruelty is only the response to what is seen as historical necessity. Justice has now passed out of the world of litigants and claimants, kingship is no longer the crowning splendor of a demi-paradise. Justice in an iron age is a matter for policemen, not for judges.

There is no need to speculate here on what happened in England during the 1590's that forced upon its two most sensitive minds such strikingly similar visions of history. Nor are Spenser and Shakespeare alone. Donne's early *Satire III* is written at this time, as are Chapman's completion to Marlowe's *Hero and Leander,* Bacon's *Essays,* and Daniel's *Musophilus.* What is striking about these works is the contrast with the great works of the previous decade: Sidney's *Arcadia,* the first three books of *The Faerie Queene,* Marlowe's plays and *Hero and Leander,* Greene's *Friar Bacon* and *James IV,* Shakespeare's early histories. The grave exuberance of Spenser, the builded moral universe of Sidney, the shouted triumph of Marlowe's plays and the playful wit of his poem, the cheerful, sympathetic complacency of Greene, the assured confidence of Shakespeare's historical vision —all these are replaced in the middle of the next decade by voices more ironic, more skeptical, more despairing, more afraid of chaos. Given this there is no reason to believe that Spenser's response in Book V is only an expression of private disappointment.

But Spenser was ten years older than Shakespeare and twenty years older than Donne, and so while they could make of impending disaster the material for their greatest work, Spenser could not. *The Faerie Queene,* the labor of a lifetime, is based on the presumption that no disaster, no pain, no monstrousness is best described *solus,* as a thing in itself; Richard III may herald the coming age when he says "I am I," but in Spenser no one is simply himself alone. Shakespeare went on to father a whole new kind of man, the refugee from Faerie Land; Hamlet lives in an unweeded garden but knows it once was weeded, he knows the earth is a sterile promontory but that it "is" or should be a goodly frame, he knows man is the quintessence of dust but also "is" or should be

the paragon of animals, the glass of fashion and the mold
of form. In such dramatic worlds the refugees become
heroic. But Spenser's imagination had not only grown
up in the older undramatic world, but it had also most
fully expressed itself there. Shakespeare makes drama out
of disaster, but Spenser could only run. So in Book VI he
tries to withdraw from the field that had so badly scarred
both him and his poem:

> *The waies, through which my weary steps I guyde,*
> *In this delightfull land of Faery,*
> *Are so exceeding spacious and wyde,*
> *And sprinckled with such sweet variety*
> *Of all that pleasant is to eare or eye,*
> *That I, nigh ravisht with rare thoughts delight,*
> *My tedious travell doe forget thereby;*
> *And when I gin to feele decay of might,*
> *It strength to me supplies, and chears my dulled*
>   *spright.*
>
>   (VI,1)

When the Red Crosse Knight thought Faerie Land
was lovely, Spenser had him cast into irons. In the middle
of Book II Spenser had beautifully described a "delight-
full land" that also was "sprinckled with such sweet
variety Of all that pleasant is to eare or eye." But in Book
II he knew that the name for such a world was Immodest
Merth and that one got there by crossing the Idle Lake.
One thing about which Spenser has always been clear is
that in Faerie Land there is no place to hide. But here he
stands, weary not of his moral intention but of the world,
trying to hide by transforming Faerie Land into something it had never been before, a place of rest for lonely,
weary, wandering travelers.

Harry Berger has a very fine account of Spenser as he appears to us in Book VI:

> The poet is bemused, a little bewildered, by the rich variety of Faerie, its many paths, the lure of so many joys. He is like all the lovers in the woods, or Timias with Belphoebe, or Arthur disarmed by his dream of Gloriana. Book VI is his Acidale, where he finds freedom from care. But at the same time the other part of his imagination realizes what is happening. The contrivance of the narrative, the inconclusiveness of the adventures, the gradual flawing of the romance world, the failure of chivalric action—these suggest that the poet is no longer certain about the ability of his imaginary forms to deal with facts of social existence.[3]

What must have bemused Spenser most was the contrast between the lovely landscapes in Book VI, filled as never before with streams and groves, and the life he found there. In the first canto we hear "a ruefull shrieke Of one loud crying," and the cry echoes through the whole book. Every lady is in distress and Calidore and Calepine continually come a moment too late to help. The delightful scene is evoked only to be marred or destroyed:

> *The faire Serena (so his lady hight)*
> *Allur'd with myldnesse of the gentle wether,*
> *And pleasaunce of the place, the which was dight*
> *With divers flowres distinct with rare delight,*
> *Wandred about the fields, as liking led*
> *Her wavefing lust after her wandring sight,*
> *To make a garland to adorne her hed,*
> *Without suspect of ill or daungers hidden dred.*

[3] "The Prospect of Imagination," *Studies in English Literature*, I (1961), 104.

All sodainely out of the forrest nere
The Blatant Beast forth rushing unaware,
Caught her thus loosely wandring here and there,
And in his wide great mouth away her bare . . .

(VI,iii,23–24)

Earlier Calidore finds Aladine lying wounded and Pris-
cilla "piteously complayning With loud laments that
most unluckie stound"; later the Salvage Man comes
on Calepine and Serena, both wounded; later still, Arthur
finds Timias wounded. These wounds, furthermore, are
nothing like the wounds of love in Books III–IV. The
wounding there, as we have seen, is constantly seen as
part of a larger process: of loving, of gracious nursing,
of monstrous sexual perversion, of courtly seduction, of
natural generation. But the wounds in Book VI are, by
comparison, only wounds: sore, grievous, impossible to
heal quickly, sometimes festering, always rendering the
wounded more helpless in the face of the next attack.
Over and over, as with a formula, Spenser returns to the
physical pain of the wounds. In Canto v,28, Serena says
she is the wretchedest dame "Who both in minde, the
which most grieveth me, And body have receiv'd a
mortall wound"; three stanzas later Spenser returns:

For now her wounds corruption gan to breed;
And eke this squire, who likewise wounded was
Of that same monster late, for lacke of heed,
Now gan to faint . . .

(VI,v,31)

Eight stanzas later he comes back again:

But faire Serene all night could take no rest,
Ne yet that gentle squire, for grievous paine

> *Of their late woundes, the which the Blatant Beast*
> *Had given them, whose griefe through suffraunce*
>   *sore increast.*
>
> (VI,v,39)

Perhaps more revealing of the flawed, rent, and helpless quality of this lovely world is the hopelessness of the
efforts of the knights to heal or of Spenser to explain.
Aladine is simply left nursing his wounds, Calepine cannot help Serena, and Arthur cannot help them or Timias
either. The nursing is sweet and courteous, but usually
to no avail, and when Spenser finally does attempt to
gather his sequence together in an explanation, he really
is at a loss. Arthur and the Salvage Man take Serena and
Timias to a hermitage and then, helplessly, move on.
Spenser then says:

> *No wound, which warlike hand of enemy*
> *Inflicts with dint of sword, so sore doth light*
> *As doth the poysnous sting, which infamy*
> *Infixeth in the name of noble wight:*
> *For by no art, nor any leaches might,*
> *It ever can recured be againe . . .*
>
> (VI,vi,1)

Since his appearance at the end of Book V, the Blatant
Beast's special quality has been the senselessness and
heedlessness of his assaults "Gainst all, both good and
bad," and the infamy of his wounds. Because the Blatant
Beast attacks any and all, the individual is powerless to
defend himself or to recover. We know why this should
be so, of course; the Blatant Beast is Spenser's distillation
of all that is senseless, infamous, slanderous, multi-
tongued, and reckless in the world around him, and he

is always bitter when he speaks of him. Faerie Land is made lovely as a place of rest and delight and courtesy, then the Beast appears, suddenly, with intent worse than mere malice or revenge, and leaves behind his victims.

But when the hermit who is to heal Serena and Timias begins to speak, he sees the matter somewhat differently:

> *'If therefore health ye seeke, observe this one.*
> *First learne your outward sences to refraine*
> *From things that stirre up fraile affection;*
> *Your eies, your eares, your tongue, your talke*
>   *restraine*
> *From that they most affect, and in due termes*
>   *containe.'*

(VI,vi,7)

Later he says: "The best . . . that I can you advize, Is to avoide the occasion of the ill." On the face of this the counsel seems to contradict the analysis of the wound, for if the Blatant Beast does strike "Gainst all, both good and bad" and leaves them "spotted with reproch, or secrete shame," then it would seem that there is nothing the victim can do about it. There is never any indication that the Beast punishes anyone for something he has done wrong, or that his victims should feel guilt for having been assaulted. It would seem then that there is nothing to be done about the Blatant Beast and that the hermit is simply offering pieties about restraint in an instance where they are particularly irrelevant.

But another way of phrasing the hermit's advice is: give up, get out, look inward, turn off your senses and your affections. Seen this way it is both appropriate and devastating. There is nothing to be done about the Blatant Beast because one cannot keep from being attacked or find cures for his bites. But because the Beast *is* a public enemy one can avoid him by becoming a hermit, by withdrawing, by refusing to look out into the world at all. In the House of Holiness in Book I withdrawal from the world was seen as a requisite to spiritual contemplation and growth, but here withdrawal is only a frail gesture of protection against a ravaging and senseless world of wounds. If this is so there can be no action, no heroism, no biding of the burden of distress, no participation in the grand and painful processes of love, no seeing or feeling at all. The best anyone can do is to give succour to the wounded; the best the wounded can do is to leave.

No wonder Calidore grows faint and leaves Faerie Land; he is only following the hermit's advice. As long as there had been battles to fight honor could be won, but the Blatant Beast is not that kind of foe. In Canto ii we learn that Calidore, as he leaves Tristram, "forth passed to his former payne," and in the next canto he beheads the wicked knight and "forth he passed thorough that daies paine." In each instance the word "pain" is like a lash because at any earlier point in the poem what here is called "pain" would have been called "task" or "quest." If that is the way Faerie Land now seems to Spenser, then the idea of leaving it must begin to seem attractive, and so Calidore goes among the shepherds and offers something hitherto unthinkable: a point of view outside Faerie Land. Meliboee's speech in Canto ix about the splendors of the pastoral life when compared to the life of the court and knight errantry contrasts what had been to this point incomparable. Faerie Land becomes a place, almost as though it could be mapped. To imagine this earlier is almost like imagining Mammon visiting the

House of Alma or Lucifera going to the castle of Malbecco.

Spenser would have us believe that this is not the
issue, and that the only question is whether shepherds
are more courteous than courtiers. We do not need to be
told, however, that the court is defective; of course courtiers live in the House of Pride and often are named
Paridell, Gardante, and Blandamour. But here Spenser's
contempt for the court is much more comprehensive and
leads him to reject *The Faerie Queene* and the whole
idea of knightly quest. Before this we have always been
aware of ambivalences in Spenser's attitude towards chivalry—he was no Malory or *Gawain* poet—but still, his
heroes are knights, his conflicts are often staged battles,
his villains are witches, wizards, and paynim knights. To
have Calidore choose to live with the shepherds is to do
far more than reveal an ideal of natural courtesy, and
Spenser, painfully honest, makes this quite clear:

> *That from henceforth he meanes no more to sew*
> *His former quest, so full of toile and paine;*
> *Another quest, another game in vew*
> *He hath, the guerdon of his love to gaine:*
> *With whom he myndes for ever to remaine,*
> *And set his rest amongst the rusticke sort,*
> *Rather then hunt still after shadowes vaine*
> *Of courtly favour, fed with light report*
> *Of every blaste, and sayling alwaies in the port.*
>
> (VI,x,2)

The wooing of Pastorella can seem a quest only to one
who has rejected chivalry. When the court becomes
"shadowes vaine" and a "painted show," Britomart and
Duessa are both rejected. The pastoral world is not a

part of Faerie Land but an alternative to it, and so here there is a real irony: Spenser takes a position which excludes him from other positions. He switches genres and chooses so that a gap is created between pastoral and Faerie. The poem itself cannot bridge the gap—when Gloriana becomes a peddler of "courtly favour" we are forced to see a figure called "Spenser himself" who bitterly makes the choice of leaving Faerie Land and going to live with the shepherds.

But Spenser was too honest and perhaps too great a man merely to run, hide, and offer fancies and goodnights. Much as he might like to do this, "Spenser himself" was too large even in defeat, and so Spenser splits "himself" into Calidore, the fleeing knightly elfin of Faerie Land, and Colin Clout, the piping lyric poet of *The Shepheardes Calender*. Colin Clout is a name Spenser gave "himself" in that earlier work, and he is there a conventional shepherd lover. Perhaps all a reader of *The Faerie Queene* needs to know about him outside of what is said in the poem is that in the "January" eclogue in the *Calender* Colin breaks his pipe because his beloved, Rosalind, "my rurall musick holdeth scorne." Here, in Canto ix, Spenser introduces him as though he were well known to all of us. We are told first that Pastorella, when she is wooed by Calidore, "cared more for Colins carolings Then all that he could doe, or ever devize." Spenser could easily have given his pastoral shepherd any name at all, and that he should have given him the name he once gave himself must call attention to a personal urgency Spenser associates with him here. In Canto ix Colin does not appear, but he exists as someone who in this pastoral world can achieve what the errant knight seeks.

In Canto x, on Mount Acidale, in one of the most touching moments in the poem, the two meet and for a moment coexist in order to show why Spenser cannot put "himself" together for longer than a moment. On the top of the Mount, Calidore finds a "troupe of ladies dauncing" and "in the midst a shepheard piping he did see." Calidore immediately fears he will break the dance if the dancers learn he is there; he sees them, but what he sees thus seems unattainable:

> . . . *even he him selfe his eyes envyde,*
> *An hundred naked maidens lilly white,*
> *All raunged in a ring, and dauncing in delight.*
>
> (VI,x,11)

In the middle of the ring three ladies are dancing, and in the middle of a ring formed by these three is a lone damsel:

> *Looke how the crowne, which Ariadne wore*
> *Upon her yvory forehead that same day*
> *That Theseus her unto his bridale bore,*
> *When the bold Centaures made that bloudy fray*
> *With the fierce Lapithes, which did them dismay,*
> *Being now placed in the firmament,*
> *Through the bright heaven doth her beams display,*
> *And is unto the starres an ornament,*
> *Which round about her move in order excellent.*
>
> (VI,x,13)

In no earlier mythology are the Centaurs and Lapithes connected in any way with Ariadne. What Spenser wants is an image in the middle of the stanza that will by its violence set off the harmonizing power of the crown in the firmament that is the lone maiden in the middle of the dance. Then Spenser makes this harmonizing ornament into a pastoral figure:

> She was, to weete, that jolly shepheards lasse,
> Which piped there unto that merry rout;
> That jolly shepheard which there piped was
> Poore Colin Clout (who knowes not Colin Clout?)
> He pypt apace, whilest they him daunst about.
> Pype, jolly shepheard, pype thou now apace
> Unto thy love, that made thee low to lout;
> Thy love is present there with thee in place,
> Thy love is there advaunst to be another Grace.
>
> (VI,x,16)

The Graces "all gifts of grace do graunt," and the maiden is here made a fourth grace; Colin is their singer. The source of order excellent, of all graces, of courtesy, is pastoral song.

But Calidore is outside this scene, and the moment he moves toward it, it disappears. The logic is inescapable; the refugee from Faerie Land, much as he might wish to, cannot join the dance that is the courteous pastoral. Calidore is left alone with Colin, who "for fell despight Of that displeasure, broke his bag-pipe quight." Nothing could better express the awful impasse Spenser has reached. As the poet of Faerie Land he seeks withdrawal from the world of the Blatant Beast, yet the moment he tries to join the world in which, as Colin, he had once lived and which he now sees as the source of all grace, the scene disappears. Because Calidore *has* fatally interrupted, because Spenser *is* Calidore's poet and the poet of Faerie, Colin can only speak in the past tense. His pipe is broken, and all he can tell Calidore is that the dancing ladies, the Graces, and the pastoral maiden

are no more and "by no meanes thou canst recall againe."
It is as though Spenser returns to himself and finds he
can no longer be a poet of Faerie or of pastoral. Spenser
looks at Spenser, his innocence gone. The trapped poet
of his mighty poem, he must wearily and forlornly
descend from Acidale after he is forgiven for having
"sought that which I mote not see."

Now that Calidore has been tolled back to his sole
self, however, even the shepherd's world is no longer the
same. The tigers and the brigands invade and, in a piece
of fierce irony, Pastorella is taken from the shepherd's
world and restored to her "rightful place" in Faerie Land.
Calidore must go back, too, of course, and Spenser with
him, to a last effort in the world:

> and let us tell
> Of Calidore, who, seeking all this while
> That monstrous beast by finall force to quell,
> Through every place, with restlesse paine and toile,
> Him follow'd by the tract of his outragious spoile.
>
> (VI,xii,22)

Calidore finally finds the Blatant Beast, who is now more
destructive than ever:

> From thence into the sacred church he broke,
> And robd the chancell, and the deskes downe threw,
> And altars fouled, and blasphemy spoke,
> And th' images, for all their goodly hew,
> Did cast to ground, whilest none was them to rew . . .
>
> (VI,xii,25)

Calidore defeats him, to be sure, and muzzles him, and
leads him through Faerie Land in triumph, but by now

we know our poet too well to think he will seek to evade,
at the last, with the simple expedient of a lie:

> *Thus was this monster, by the maystring might*
> *Of doughty Calidore, supprest and tamed,*
> *That never more he mote endammadge wight*
> *With his vile tongue, which many had defamed,*
> *And many causelesse caused to be blamed:*
> *So did he eeke long after this remaine,*
> *Untill that, whether wicked fate so framed,*
> *Or fault of men, he broke his yron chaine,*
> *And got into the world at liberty againe.*
>
> (VI,xii,38)

Spenser neither knows nor cares how the Blatant Beast
gets loose again; after all this, he is left with only his
bitterness. The moral nihilism of the Blatant Beast is
finally triumphant in a Faerie Land that had for so long
been able to avoid simplification of this kind and to place
good and evil in its sequence in many and varied ways.
The high hopes expressed in the letter to Raleigh, the
dreams of writing twelve and even twenty-four books and
of fashioning a gentleman, the buoyant aspiration to
make wonder into religion—all these lead to this weary
and painful close:

> *Ne may this homely verse, of many meanest,*
> *Hope to escape his venemous despite,*
> *More then my former writs, all were they cleanest*
> *From blamefull blot, and free from all that wite,*
> *With which some wicked tongues did it backebite,*
> *And bring into a mighty peres displeasure,*
> *That never so deserved to endite.*
> *Therfore do you, my rimes, keep better measure,*

> *And seeke to please, that now is counted wisemens*
>   *threasure.*
>
> (VI,xii,41)

Only the archaic spelling is left; rhetoric here seeks nothing like persuasion. The "now" is spit out, and toward the foolish "wisemen" who seek of his poem only that it please.

What is perhaps most moving here is that Spenser offers no solace to any part of him that wished to pretend. His poem has come crashing down around him and he solemnly and bitterly insists there is no other way.

❧

After Spenser, the deluge. His is the last major work in English to imagine a world both whole and harmonious with anything like the serenity of vision that a vitally whole and harmonious culture could provide. What Spenser "knew," in one sense, men have gone on knowing ever since, but the emphasis was altered radically during the poet's own lifetime, and "knowing" would never again seem the same. The vast and experimental labor that is Shakespearean drama proved decisive; Calidore is only forlorn at the end of Book VI, unable to respond to the disaster of his world's failure. But Hamlet shudders and lurches off to set right the time that can never again be set right. Troilus speaks in the debate of Helen as a "theme of honor and renown, A spur to valiant and magnanimous deeds," and so can praise Hector for having touched the life of the great Trojan design. But this elfin spirit is smashed and he ends cursing the abominable Greek tents, nursing the hope for revenge. Only a few years later Lear, no longer interested in the mere placement of self in a disordered world, seeks to bring that whole world down in scorn, thunder, and punishment for its chaos; in his wake he leaves unaccommodated man, a naked figure crying on the great stage of fools. Read with *The Faerie Queene* behind it, Shakespeare's career takes on strange and brilliant lights, for we can, coming from Faerie Land, see how immensely daring, original, and courageous he was in letting it all come down and making his drama thereby. Though no one at the time could possibly have known or felt it, we can see that in many ways the poetry of Donne, Jonson, and Herbert is an effort to pour the wild Shakespearean wine into lyric bottles, and we can go so far as to insist that these poets wrote their best poems when they had—whatever their doctrines or "beliefs"—turned away from the serenity of Spenserian vision and towards the restless anguish of Shakespeare.

Milton would have had it differently. Beginning his career as a writer of metaphysical verse and constantly under the influence of Shakespeare, he tried to move away. He knew well enough to know that for him Spenser was a greater teacher than Aquinas, but also that he could not simply turn himself into a Spenserian after the fashion of minor poets like the brothers Fletcher. But *Paradise Lost* can only *seek* status as a visionary and undramatic work; the time had since passed when a poet who sought to express the truths of his culture could achieve it. The very fact that a poem had to be written to justify the ways of God to man, something Spenser never would have dreamed of having to do, is in itself indicative. In Spenser we need feel no split between the sensual and the moral, but in Milton we feel it everywhere, and even sense that he felt it too. Paradise is Eden but it is also a Bower of Bliss, and so, lest Adam and Eve become Acrasia and Verdant, Milton makes them laborers in a vineyard that is in constant need of pruning. It is Satan who knows best how to respond to the splendors of Paradise; it is Michael who knows of redemption and the paradise within, happier far. The two can never speak in the same voice. Most devastating and most moving, Adam as he falls must choose as no one in Faerie Land ever did: God *or* Eve. To see how far we have come in the seventy years since *The Faerie Queene* we need only see that this choice would be analogous in the earlier poem to Scudamour's having to choose between Amoret and Venus.

After Milton it was to him that later poets turned for their image of the earlier hero in the way Milton turned to Spenser; it was Milton, not Spenser, that Blake, Wordsworth, and Shelley felt behind them as the noble watchman of the truth. They were forced into even more radical positions than Milton in their efforts to bespeak that truth: Blake transformed the world into an invented mythology always on the verge of private language, Wordsworth wrote best only when he kept his vision the matter of autobiography, Shelley never really found a myth or a language in which he could articulate his immortal longings. And after the Romantics the attempt to maintain vision for longer than a lyric effectively passes out of English poetry.

To speak this way is only to attempt to show the kind of light the reader of Spenser can cast on later literature, and the judgments laid out so flatly here of course would need to be modified by many other points of view before they could have any claim to fullness. But even this swift a survey can reveal the way in which someone who dismisses *The Faerie Queene* will probably do so to his own peril as a literary historian. The two most influential historians, Eliot and Leavis, both could not be bothered with Spenser and so they tended to praise exclusively those poets and dramatists whose language aspired to the concrete, "spoken" richness of Shakespeare. Because Shakespeare *was* decisive this mistaken assumption did not really prove disastrous, but its limits can all be laid to an inability to see what poetry can do when it is not Shakespearean. Spenser's influence on later poetry can hardly be said to be beneficial, and when Eliot and Leavis saw that, they drew the erroneous and unhistorical conclusion that the fault must be Spenser's. Obviously, when a poet without the richness of Spenser's vision tries to write "like Spenser," he will almost always end up being languorous, decorative, plaintive. The best poems in Spenserian stanzas after Spenser—*Childe Harold's Pilgrimage, Adonais, The Eve of St. Agnes*—all suffer from these qualities and represent vices their authors had to fight free from in order to achieve their best work. Byron, Shelley, Keats, and all other poets who began their careers under the "influence of Spenser" had to liberate themselves from him before they wrote well.

But no one who has been carefully through *The Faerie Queene* need be misled by this use of Spenser by later poets. Our sense of history and literary influence is narrow indeed if we need to find fault with an author because his effect on later authors was generally deleterious. What Spenser could write in 1590 was, as we have seen, simply not writable after Shakespeare. Still many poets, especially while young, could misunderstand Spenser by misunderstanding his historical position, and could proceed to do with Faerie Land what Spenser tried to do with it at the beginning of Book VI—transform it into a delightful place, a fantasy world of knights and bowers. "Deep in the shady sadness of a vale," is the first line of Keats' *Hyperion,* and a very Spenserian line it is. But Keats wanted to imagine that shady sadness precisely because it was an alternative to his own world, because in that vale he would not be rebuked as he was later implicitly rebuked by the urn and the nightingale and left with a burning forehead and a parching tongue. It is part of Keats' "maturing," we say, that Keats learned to live with his world and to recognize that the magic casements that charmed him were in fairy lands lost to him. Spenser, though, had he written of the shady sadness of a vale, never would have imagined it as an alternative place where one could go and thereby avoid going somewhere else. There aren't, at least before Book VI, any "places" at all in Faerie Land in this sense. But the Romantics and the succeeding generations bred on Romantic poetry could not see this, and so they made of Spenser what they tended to make of themselves: nostalgic sensualists who often lurched from this nostalgia into rigid morality.

Having come this far with Spenser, though, we should be able to see that Spenser is a would-be sensualist and a rigid moralist only at the end, when the serene complexity of his earlier vision had collapsed and the desperate and simplifying searches of Books V and VI left him with little else to be. We can see, too, looking back at the earlier parts of the poem, the way that it *is* all of a piece before the last two books. We can make a list of the great sequences and of the dullest stretches, but as we do we also recognize that neither list is possible without prior recognition and understanding of what C. S. Lewis once called "the seamless variety of the whole." We have seen that when the sequence is firmly in control almost everything goes right—and so seeing we *can* point to the cantos whose interest is inexhaustible: for me the list would include Cantos vii–x of Book I (Duessa-Orgoglio-Una-Arthur-Despair-Holiness), the middle of Book II (Cymochles-Phaedria) and the Bower of Bliss, almost all of Book III, Canto vi of Book IV (Britomart and Artegall), the last three cantos of Book IV (Temple of Venus-Thames and Medway-Marinell and Florimell). Such a list, highly selective though it is, and ignoring though it does many short and stunning passages, describes a body of poetry of over ten thousand lines, a massive achievement. But of course there is no such body and an anthology of these passages alone could not possibly do justice to the poem; they are only the moments that one returns to most often after the whole has been read many times. We need not only the rest of the first four books to show us why these are perhaps the best things in the poem, but also the inferior final two books to allow us to see the whole in any genuine perspective.

For in the last analysis we can only be just to Spenser if we recognize what the inevitable motions of history did to *The Faerie Queene* and to our ability to read it rightly. If the argument of this book is at all valid, this recognition does not in the least require that we cease to maintain our citizenship in the twentieth century; indeed, the poem has been most injured by those who have sought to renounce that citizenship. It does require, however, that we understand that Spenser can most live for us if we remember that his world was ending as he was writing. History, visible history, is happening in the last two books; the world is reaching one of its major turning points, and the world described near the end of the poem is much closer than is anything earlier to what we sometimes call "modern life." Nearly a century later Thomas Hobbes looked back on that moment and said that in 1588 his mother gave birth to two children, himself and fear. Spenser felt that fear and did his best to make his poem, shaped as it was for other purposes, to respond to it. In his failure lies perhaps our best chance to understand his earlier success. When the hermit in Book VI says he cannot cure the wounds of the Blatant Beast and that therein the mind must minister unto itself, he expresses a sense of life we can embrace and simultaneously he makes us remember earlier, different moments. When Arthur rescues the Red Crosse Knight from Orgoglio's prison he says:

> *This daies ensample hath this lesson deare*
> *Deepe written in my heart with yron pen,*
> *That blisse may not abide in state of mortall men.*
>
> (I,viii,44)

But his is an heroic comfort, an acknowledgment of fallenness and humanity that contains within it the belief that awareness of the human condition should lead not to despair but to battle, and with dragons and flames.

Arthur is not a denizen of "modern life"; the split is there and we must recognize it. But to say this is not to say that we cannot understand him, or that he is irrelevant to us. His heroism and his creator's assurance are *there,* densely imagined human possibilities, and only one with little understanding and an extremely narrow sense of relevance can dismiss this. We seek justice for Spenser because we seek the best he knows, and in finding that best we see that though he is astringently alien, he can show us he knows the glory and pain of living. Beautifully, the more we can see that he is not like us, the more we can discover that he is.

Index

The Index of Passages Discussed is limited to those in which more than passing reference is made. The Index of Characters and Places includes all references.

Passages Discussed

Characters and Places